How To Draw People

People

Learn to create human form in a DAY!

by Elissa Reyes

Copyright©2015 Elissa Reyes

Table of Contents

Disclaimer

While all attempts have been made to verify the information provided in this book, the author does assume any responsibility for errors, omissions, or contrary interpretations of the subject matter contained within. **The information provided in this book is for educational and entertainment purposes only. The reader is responsible for his or her own actions and the author does not accept any responsibilities for any liabilities or damages, real or perceived, resulting from the use of this information.**

The trademarks that are used are without any consent, and the publication of the trademark is without permission or backing by the trademark owner. All trademarks and brands within this book are for clarifying purposes only and are the owned by the owners themselves, not affiliated with this document.

Introduction

Have you ever watched a carpenter as he hangs an entryway. He makes it look so natural, this is on the grounds that he has gained the abilities to do it easily throughout the years.

As the carpenter spent time learning the abilities he has learning how to draw portraits just requires a little guideline and a lot of practice.

Try not to take a gander at an incredible portrait and contrast your own particular abilities and the craftsman's who drew it, this will just dishearten you. The craftsman will have had years of experience, yet he would have been similarly situated you are in toward the starting

.

Learning to draw portraits is only an aptitude and you have to learn the abilities gradually, beginning from the basics. On the off chance that you were beginning to learn how to play the violin, no one would anticipate that you will get up and begin playing at symphonic standard following a couple of hours. It's the same when you are learning how to draw, you can't hope to turn out fabulous pictures to start with.

Portrait drawing is an incredible subject on the grounds that we as individuals are captivating and every head contains so much that people are drawn to portrait drawing. Aside from that think the amount of fun it would be to have the capacity to draw awesome portraits of your crew.

To learn how to draw portraits start with the basics and develop gradually. Practice is the way to learning how to draw. Keep in mind don't hope to be creating extraordinary drawings straight away, no one ever delivers a gem with their initial work. Your first drawings won't be great, that is fine, they're not intended to be.

Portrait drawing can be separated into little parts, you have to learn how to draw the human head, eyes, ears and hair. Each requires great perception and a lot of practice. Your practice drawings are not intended to be perfect works of art. They're your scratchpad, you're learning scrawls.

Learning how to draw portraits requires a touch of guideline and a lot of practice. The magnificence about learning to draw is that you can hone it anyplace.

Everything you need is a journal and a pencil in the first place. You can then practice in any extra minute you have. while sitting tight for a transport, amid your break at work, for all intents and purposes anyplace.

The most ideal approach to learn to portrait draw is to do it from life by inspiring somebody to posture for you for some time. A relative is normally cheerful to oblige. Coming up short that you can hone from photographs or get a wooden puppet to put around your work area or table. What's imperative is that you practice and practice.

Chapter 1 – How to draw a girl

Step 1: In this stride what you will be doing is drawing out the body edge and rules for the young ladies body. Beginning at the head draw an oval shape for the head then draw the facial rules to ensure the eyes and nose turn out symmetrical.

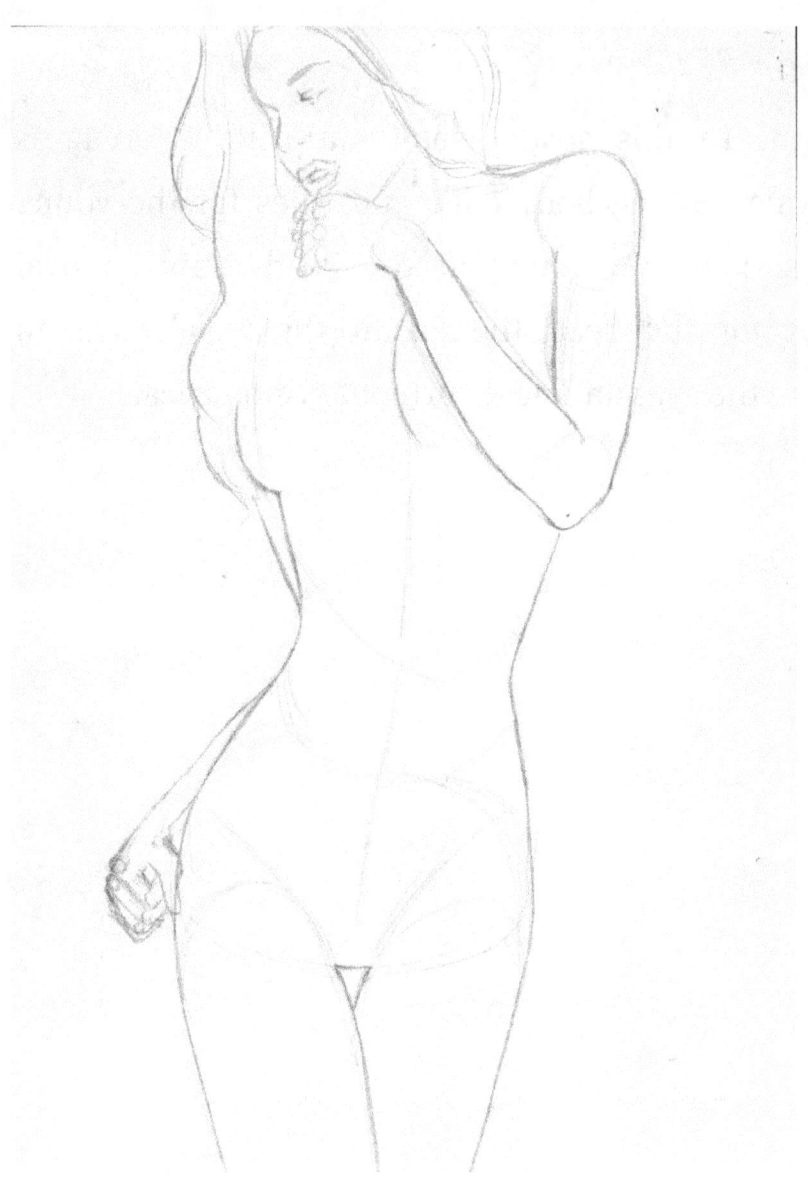

Step 2: Next draw a line for the neckline bone and shoulders, from the end of that line draw both arms

then elbow circles and after that hand guides. Draw out the pelvis and long appendage lines with the foot shapes to finish this stride.

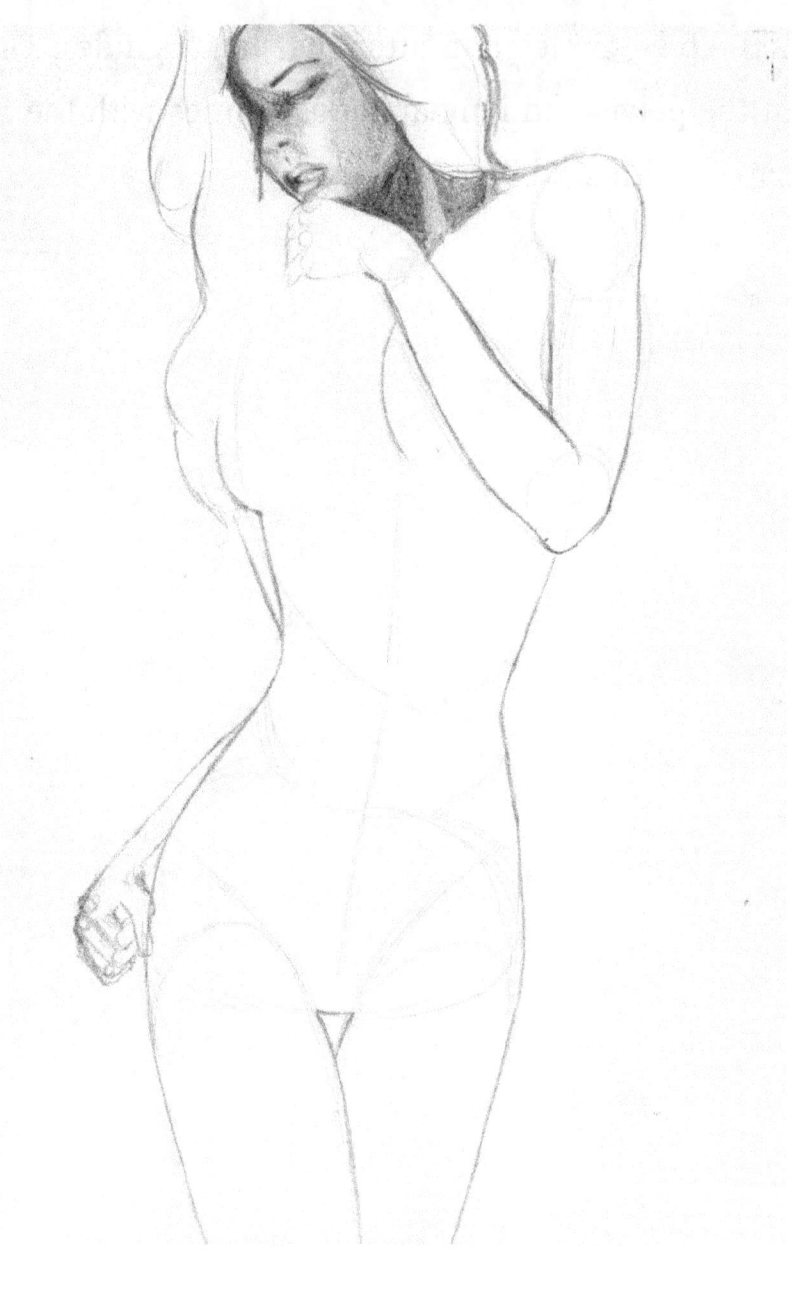

Step 3: In this stride you will be sketching out the eyes, I sketched them to look enormous and lovely, and the eyebrows are simply little angled lines. Sketch a little nose and the lip lines.

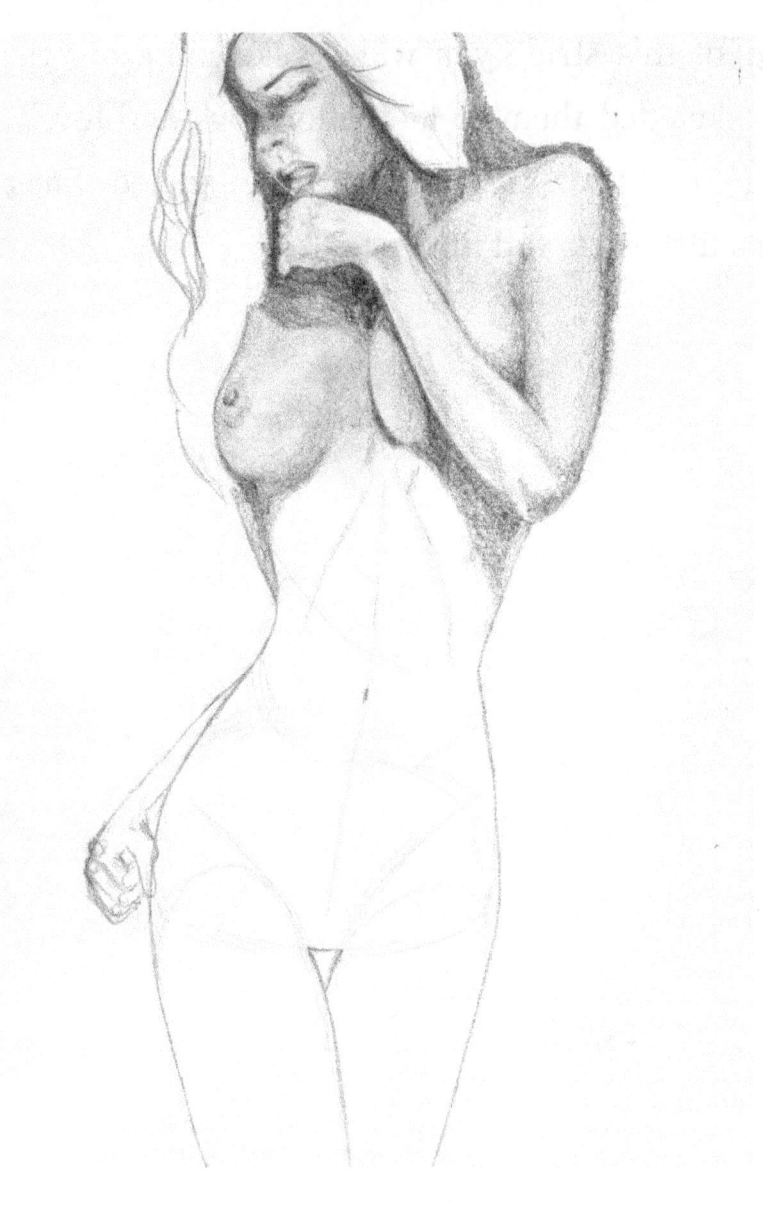

Step 4: On the middle some portion of the aide, you can sketch in her bust and panty outfit best that wraps around the neck.

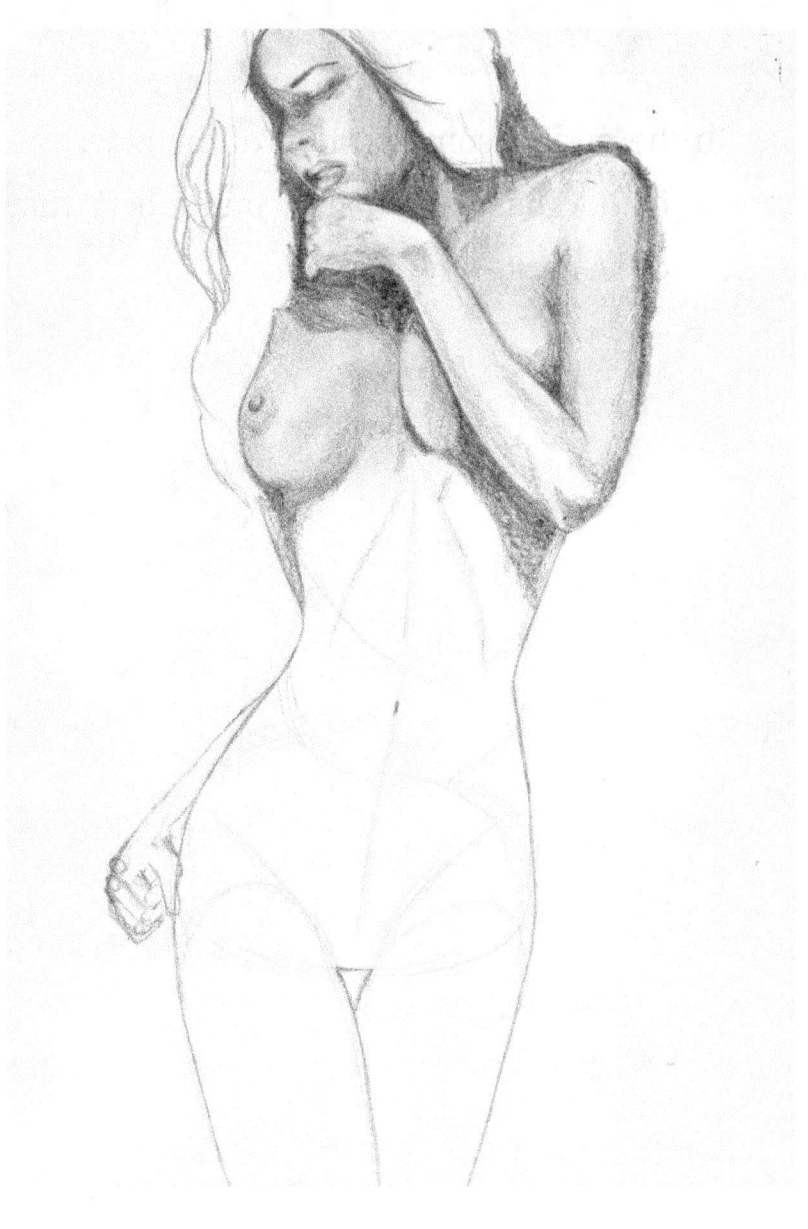

Step 5: Draw out her top appendages and hands, then draw out her shapely waist. As should be obvious the provocative awful young lady is looking better with every stride that passes. Before moving to the following step sketch in the top some portion of her thighs.

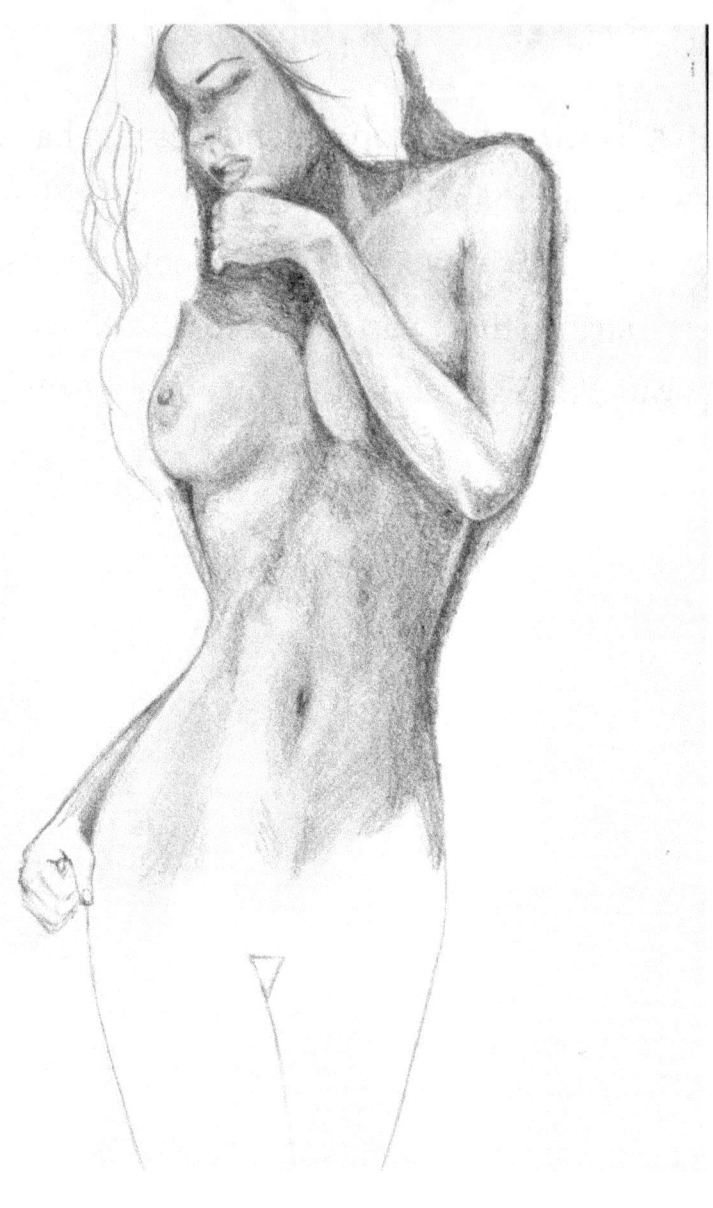

Step 6: As you probably are aware this is the last step, and what dependably accompanies last steps?

Step 7: Complete the process of sketching in her face and take as much time as is needed sketching and drawing her long excellent hair. The hair is thick long pieces to make it simpler to draw.

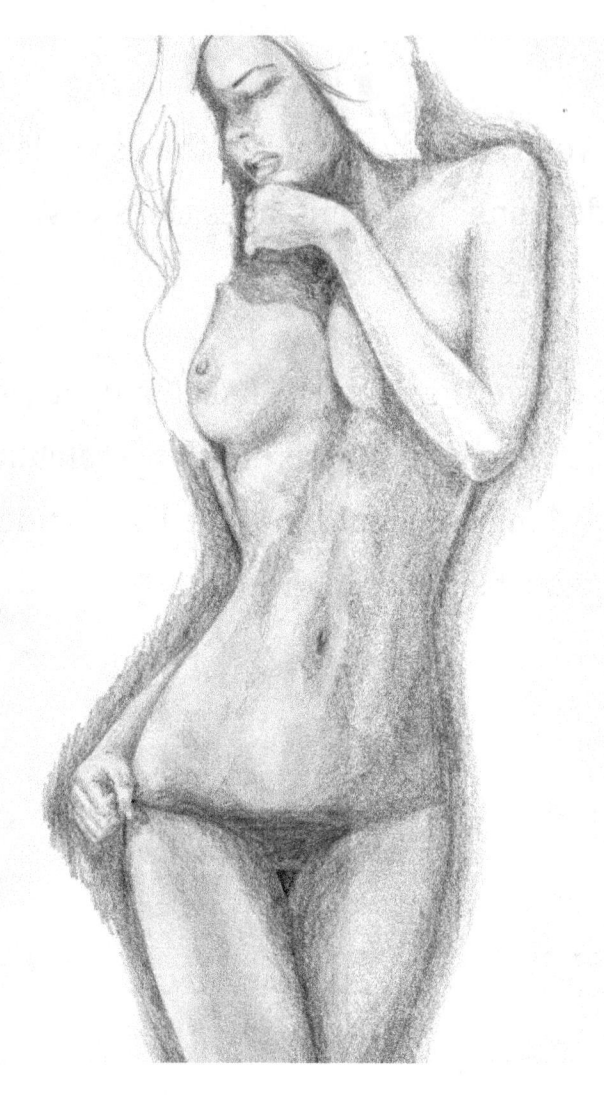

Step 8: After you wrap up her hair, complete the sketch by drawing in whatever remains of her legs and feet. I truly needed her to look sound rather than a wiped out thin. After you does all that eradicate every one of the rules and sketch checks and move onto the following step.

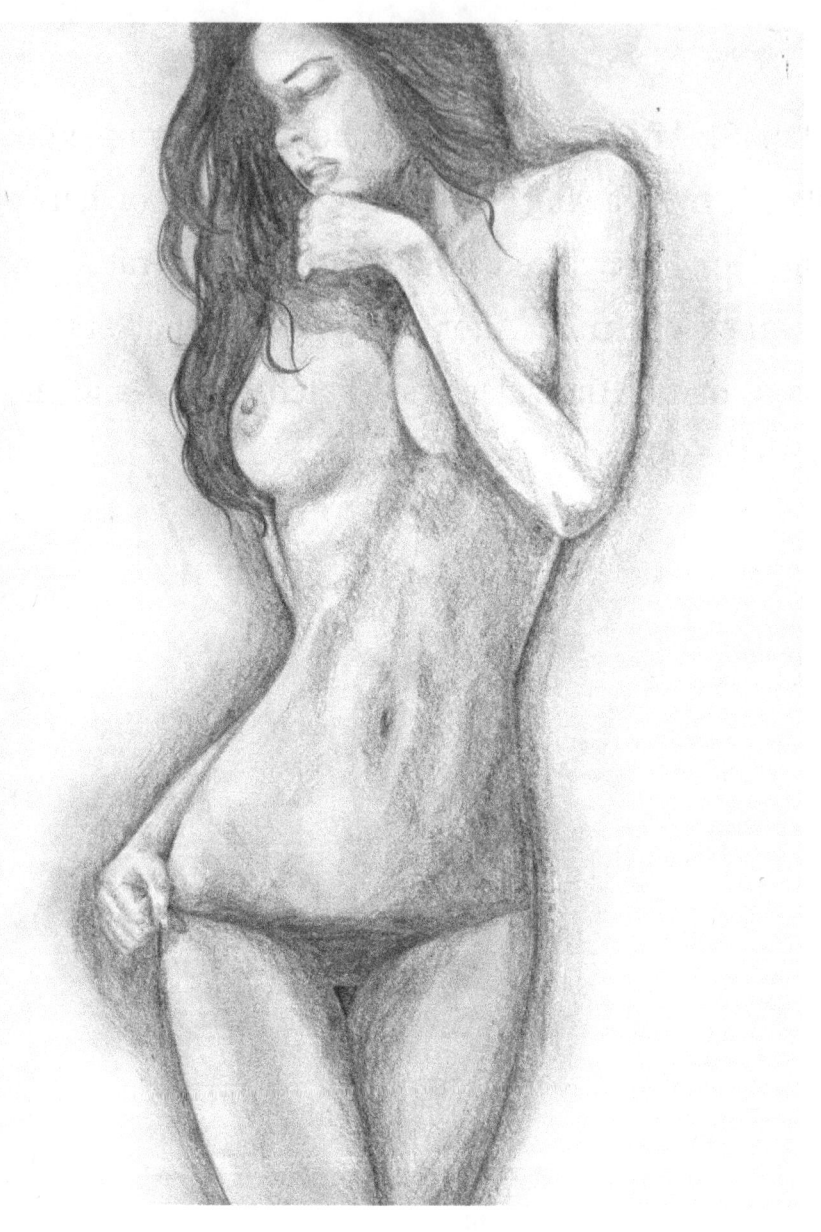

Step 9: This is your last step. What's more, what you
need to is shading her in. You can give her fair hair

and a blue or dark swimming outfit, whatever you need you can do.

Chapter 2 – How to draw girl 2

Step 1: You'll need drawing paper with an unpretentious unpleasantness that will permit mediums like charcoal to stick and stay set up, charcoal, delicate pencils, square colored pencils, and erasers.

Step 2: Mull over what parts of her body you'd like to concentrate on.

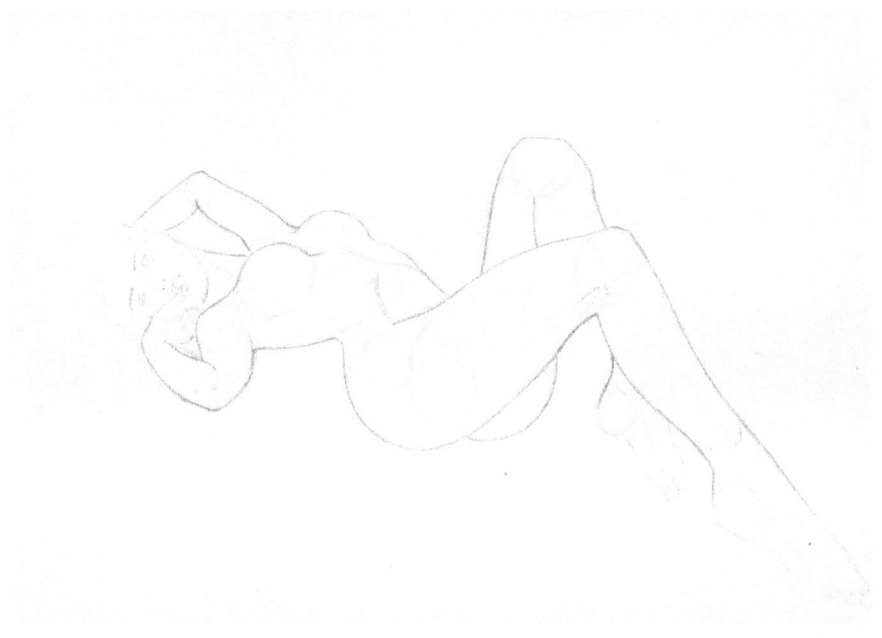

Step 3: Work out extents Work out extents utilizing the 'thumb and pencil' strategy. Standing 10 feet from your model, hold a pencil in your outstretched hand and, utilizing your predominant eye, line it up with the highest point of her head. Presently move your finger down the pencil until you go to her jaw—that is her head estimation.

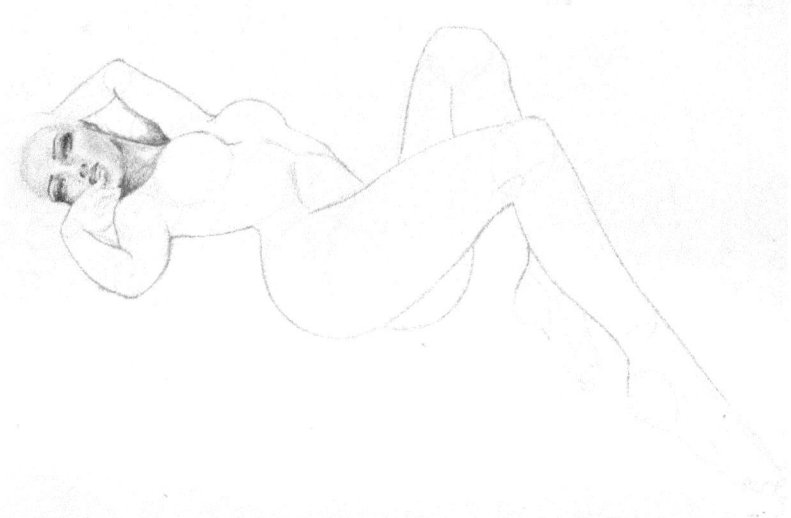

Step 4: Measure stature Still utilizing the pencil, make sense of what number of "heads" tall she is.

Step 5: Determine body estimations Armed with the head estimation, utilize the accompanying aide for body extents: stature = 8 heads; neck = ¼ head; shoulder width = 2 heads; bosoms to gut = 1 head.

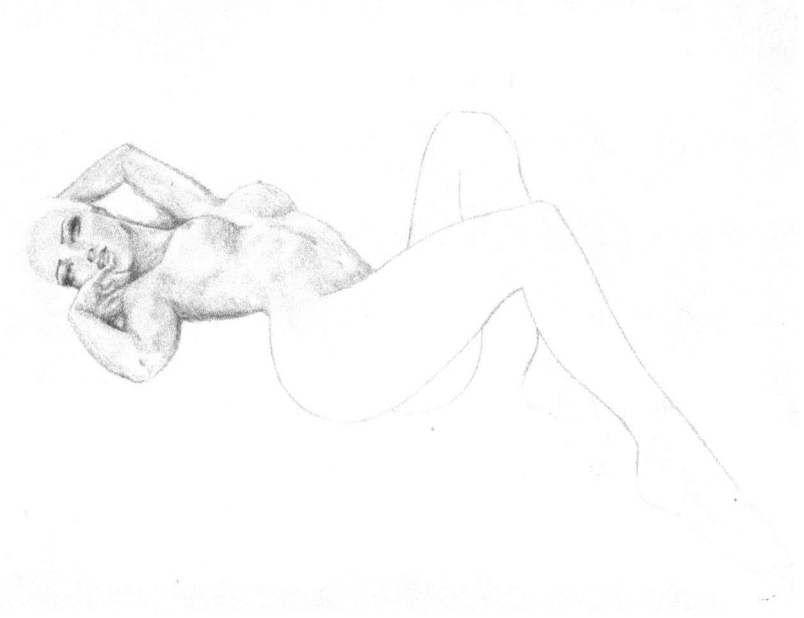

Step 6: Study her body Study her body before you begin to draw. (Yes, this is one time where it's superbly satisfactory to gaze brazenly at an exposed lady.) Note how her body meets up at joints, and what lines stress what body parts.

Step 7: Start to draw Let your eyes move over the shapes of her body while your hand draws what you see. Your eyes ought to be taking in every curve and edge—the way her hair falls, the curve of her back, the state of her mouth and eyes.

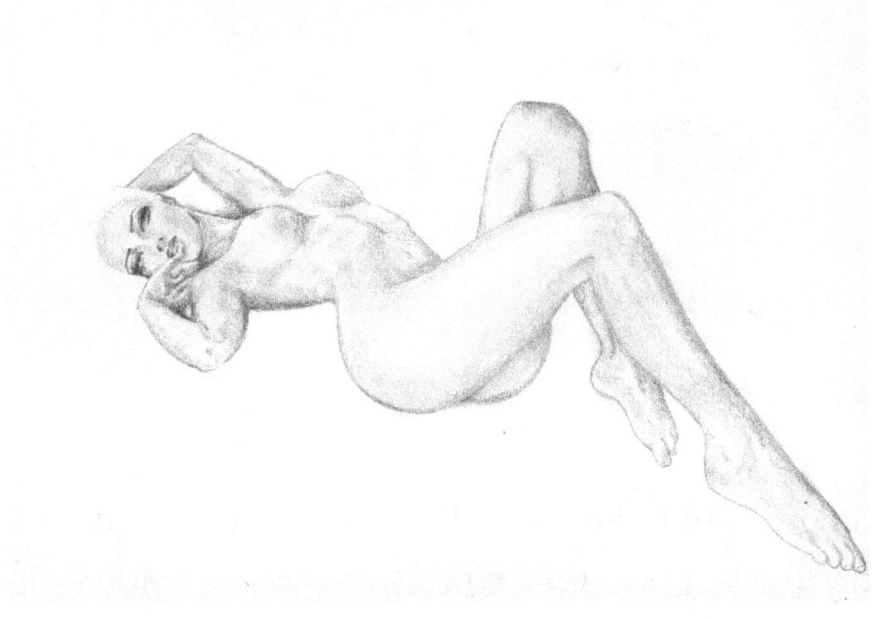

Step 8: Draw in quick lines Break your figure down to straightforward lines that you draw quickly—don't submit your pencil to the page for more than a few moments.

Step 9: Use shadow and light Use the charcoal to stress how shadow and light fall on the subject. Does the position of her body cast a shadow behind her or legs? Charcoal is the least demanding to spread and passes on shadow splendidly.

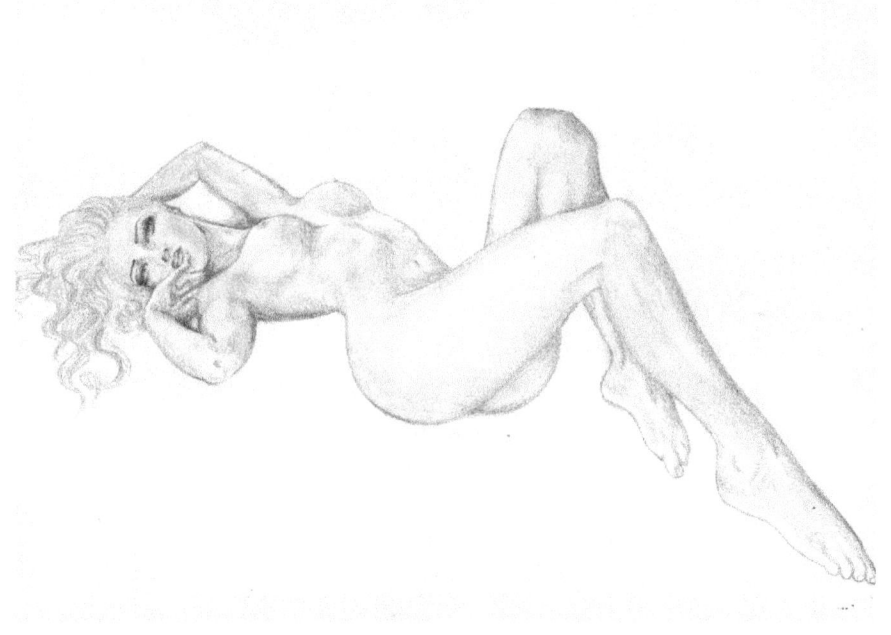

Step 10: Refine the edges with erasers. Smear where shade ought to be strengthened and eradicate where ranges ought to be helped.

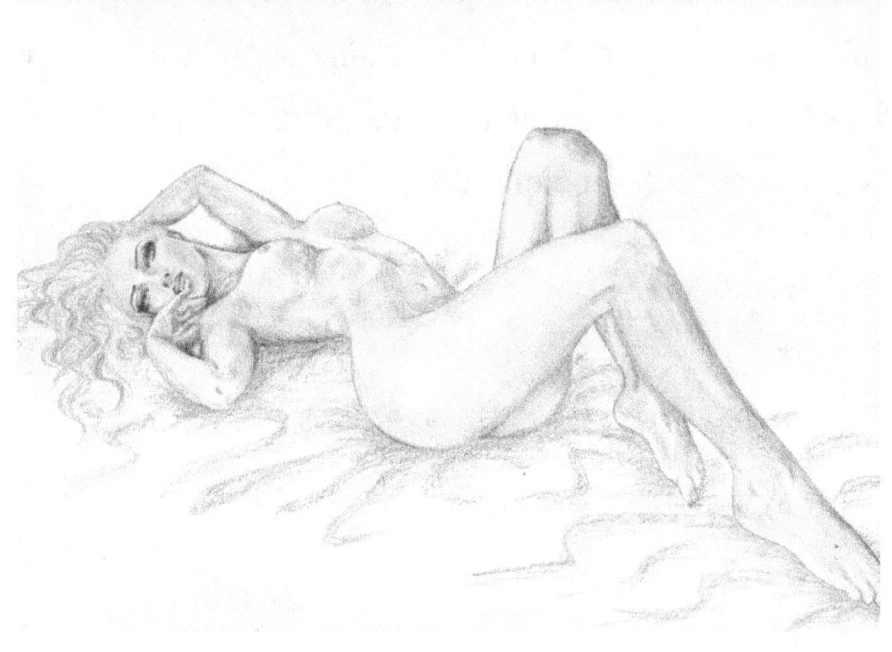

Step 11: Spray If you worked in a smirch capable medium like charcoal or delicate pencil, splash your magnum opus with fixative—a fluid varnish that will keep it from.

Chapter 3 – How to draw a nude couple

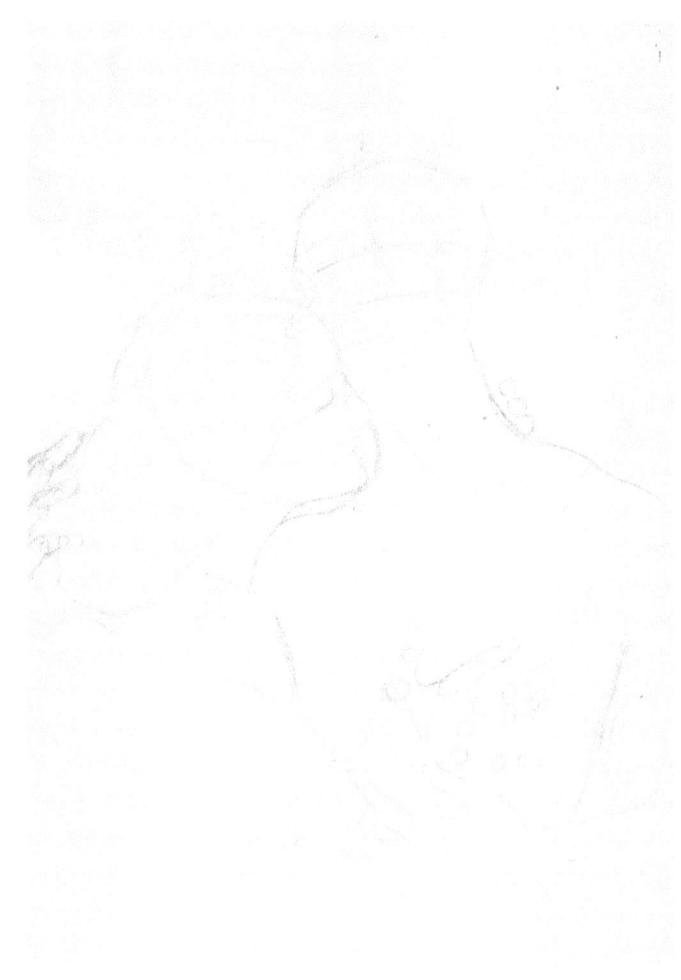

Step 1: Draw the framework sketches. Sketch two ovals somewhat crossing one another. These are the framework sketches for the necks.

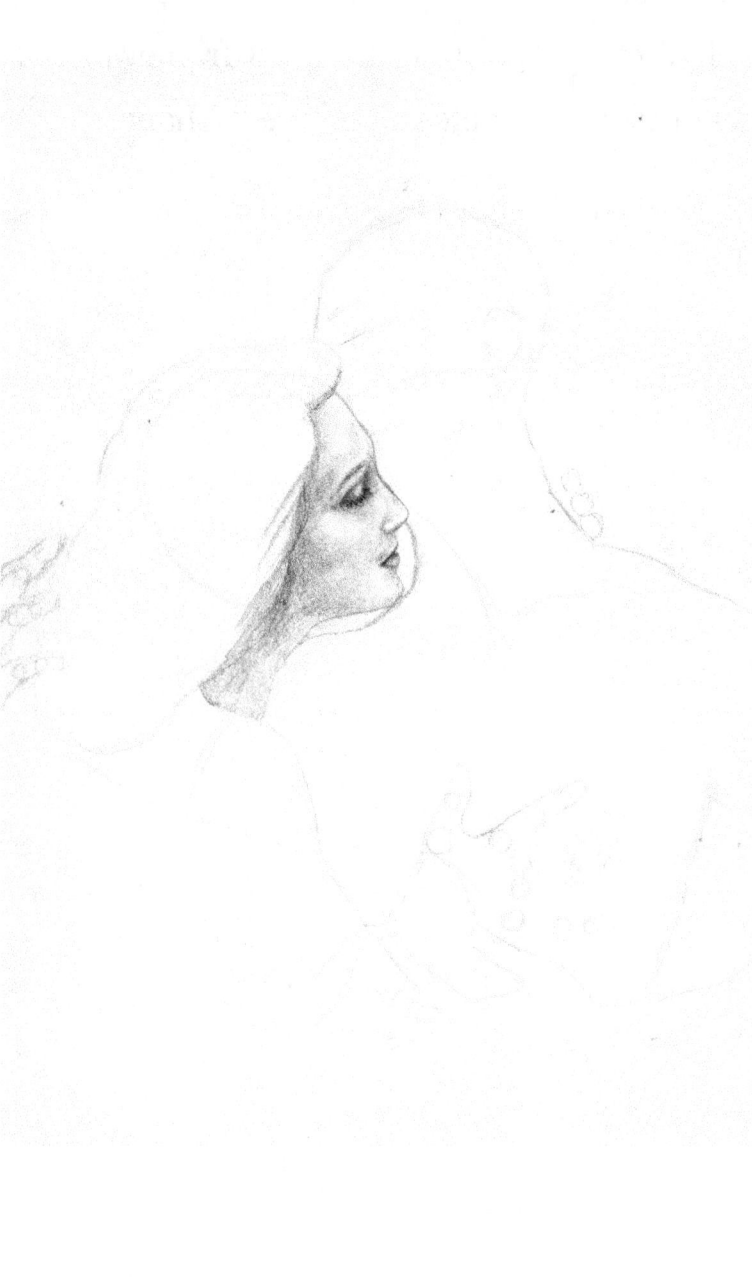

Step 2: Include the jawline profile perspective of the first character. This time the head framework of the first character resembles an oak seed shape.

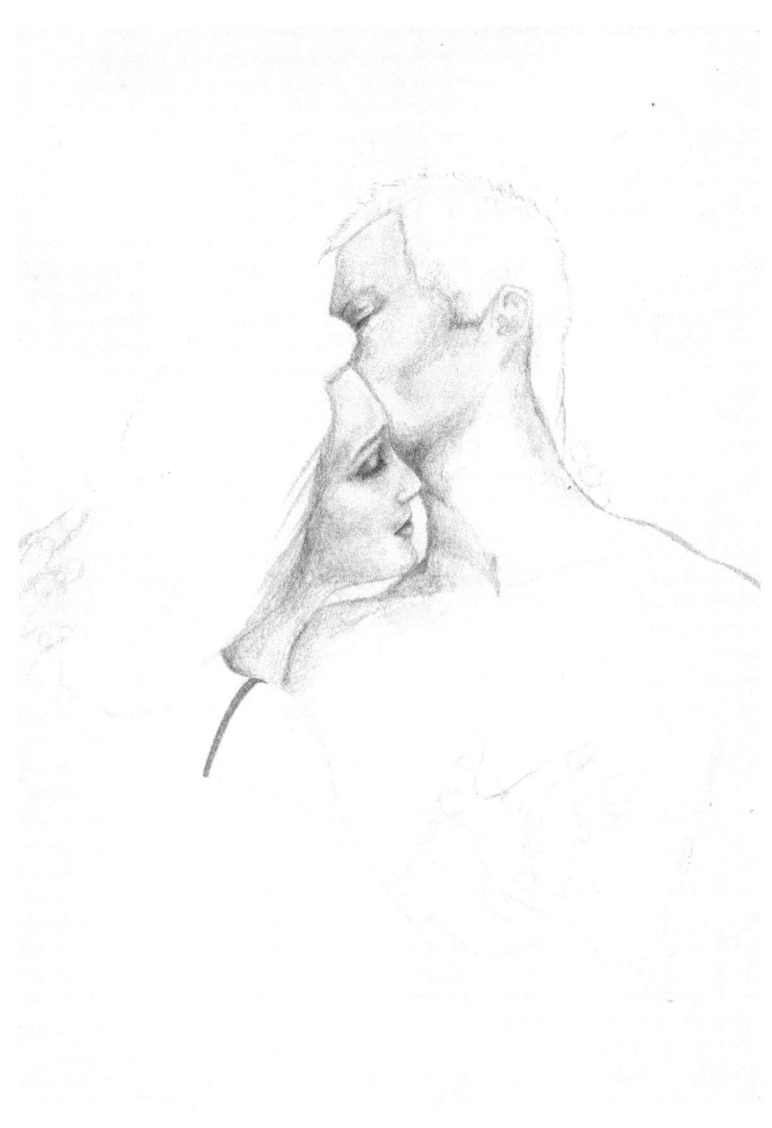

Step 3: Proceed with the jawline of the second character. In the event that you see the heart shape for the entire of the two heads traces.

Step 4: Draw the skeleton diagram. The reason for the skeleton blueprints is to guide you in drawing the body stance and sythesis. Attempt to suspect how you need their body posture to resemble.

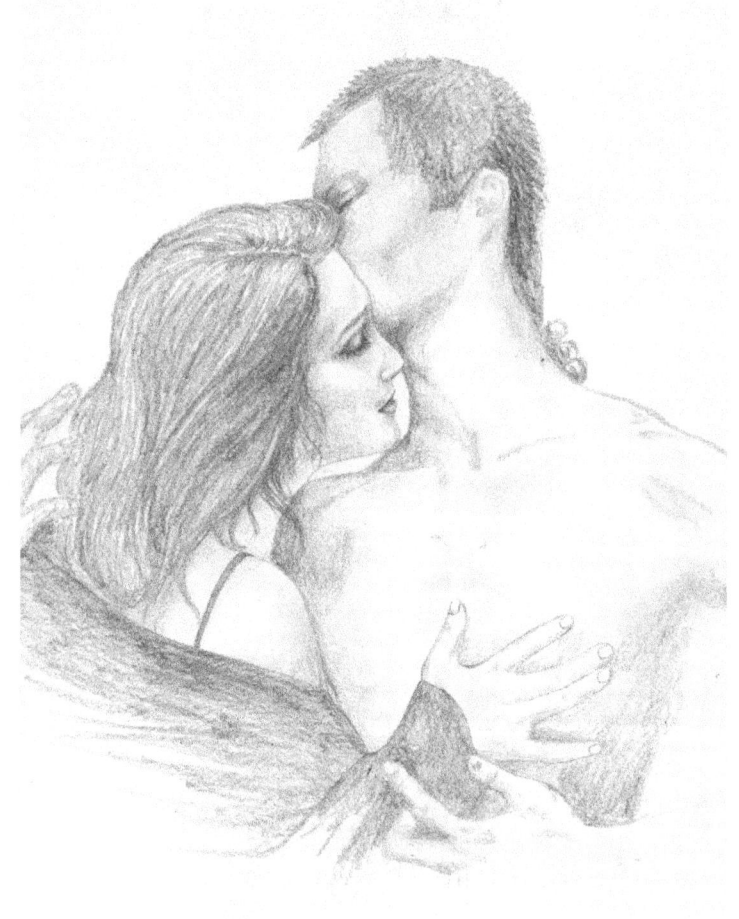

Step 5: Include the skeleton diagram for the second character. Utilizing the same procedures, include the skeleton diagrams for the second characters.

Step 6: Draw the facial element diagrams. Draw curves four vertical lines and one flat line on each of the face to demonstrate the rules for the facial component.

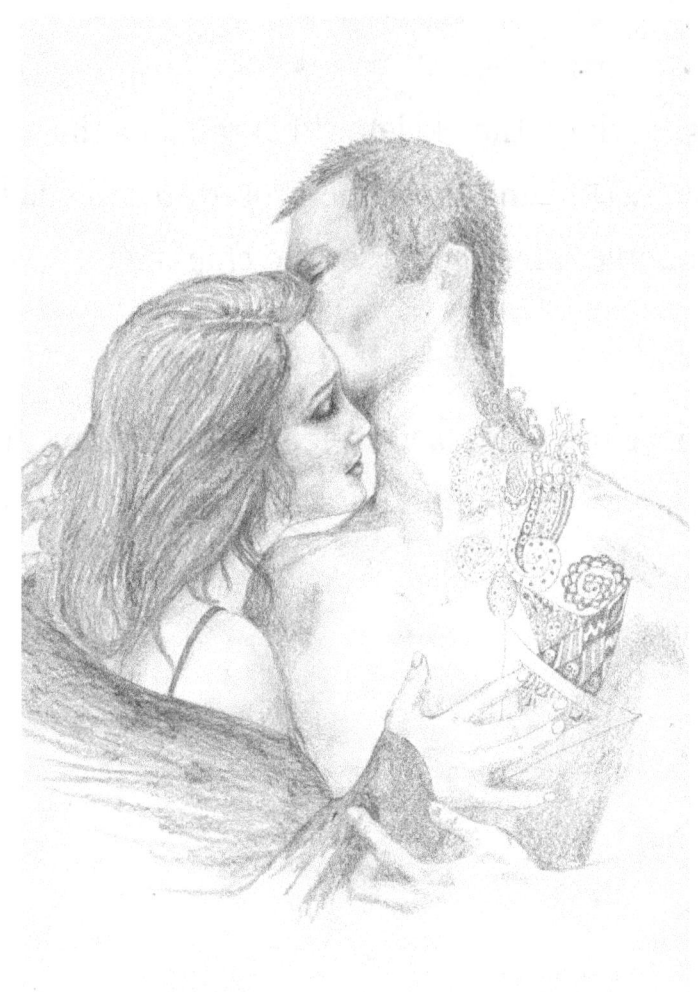

Step 7: Eradicate a percentage of the framework sketches and begin drawing the real lines for the countenances in view of the layouts.

Chapter 4 – How to draw a girl

Step 1: Sketch a circle for the head and a little elliptical for the body.

Step 2: Sketch the rules for the face and additionally the button and the jaw line.

Step 3: Include the furthest points (arms and the legs).

Step 4: Sketch her lips in a darker shading.

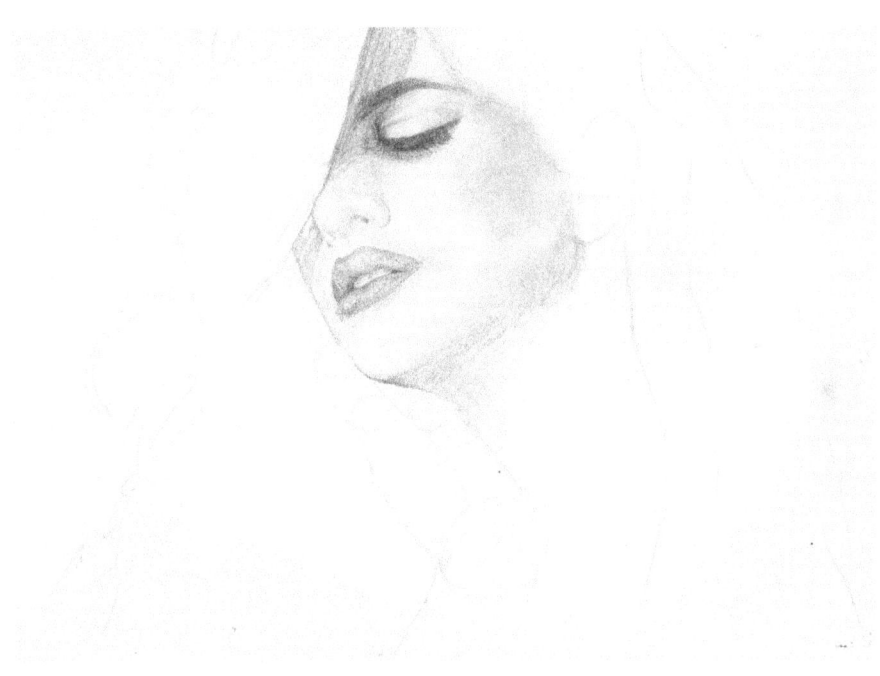

Step 5: Sketch the draft of the hair. It depends on you.

Step 6: Sketch the fundamental draft for the young lady's garments.

Step 7: Sketch alternate subtle elements of the uniform.

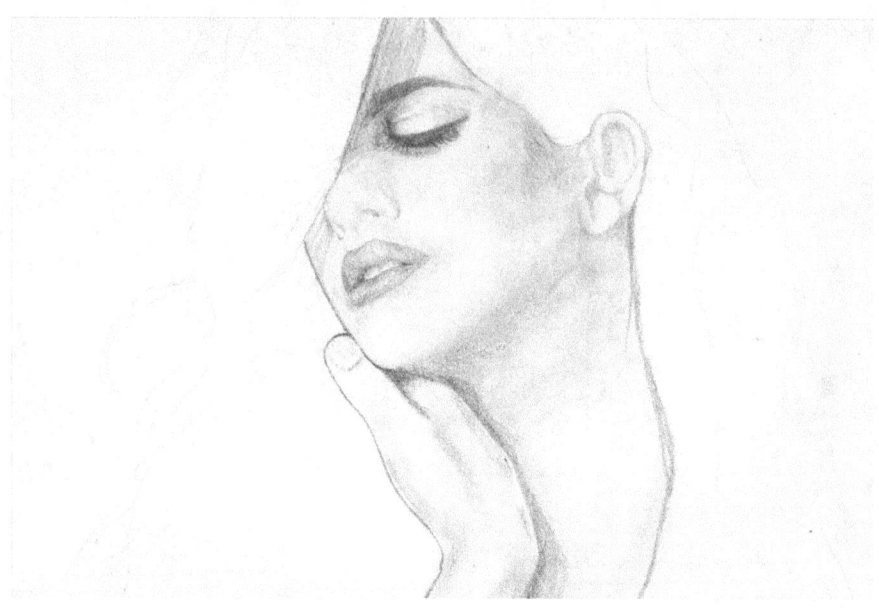

Step 8: Draw the fundamental layout of the young lady.

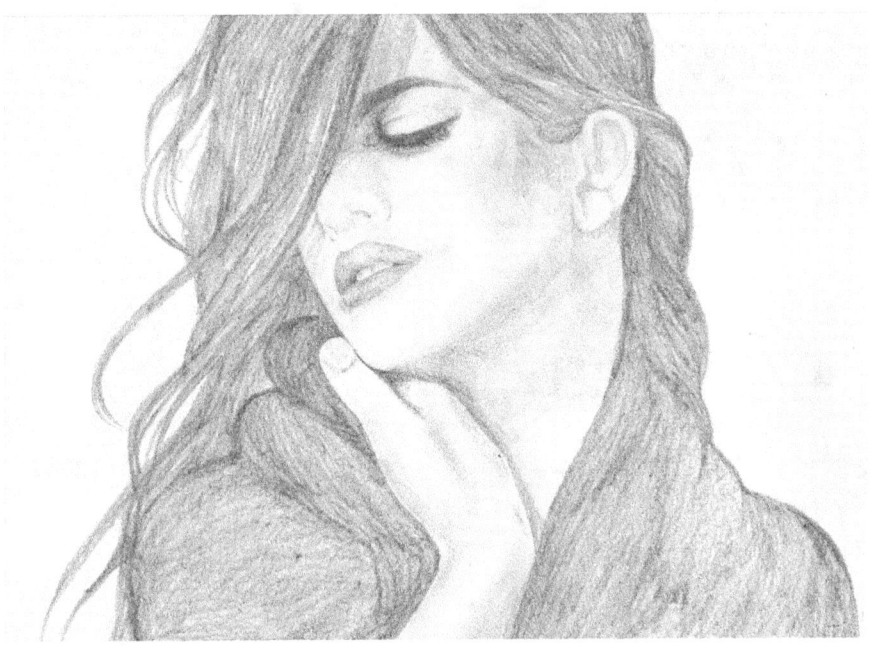

Step 9: Eradicate the draft and put in more points of interest.

Chapter 5 – How to draw a couple hugging each other

Step 1: Start with two head aides and after that draw the necks and afterward their backs.

Step 2: Begin with the kid and sketch out his untidy haircut. Include some long strands and in addition some muddled ones.

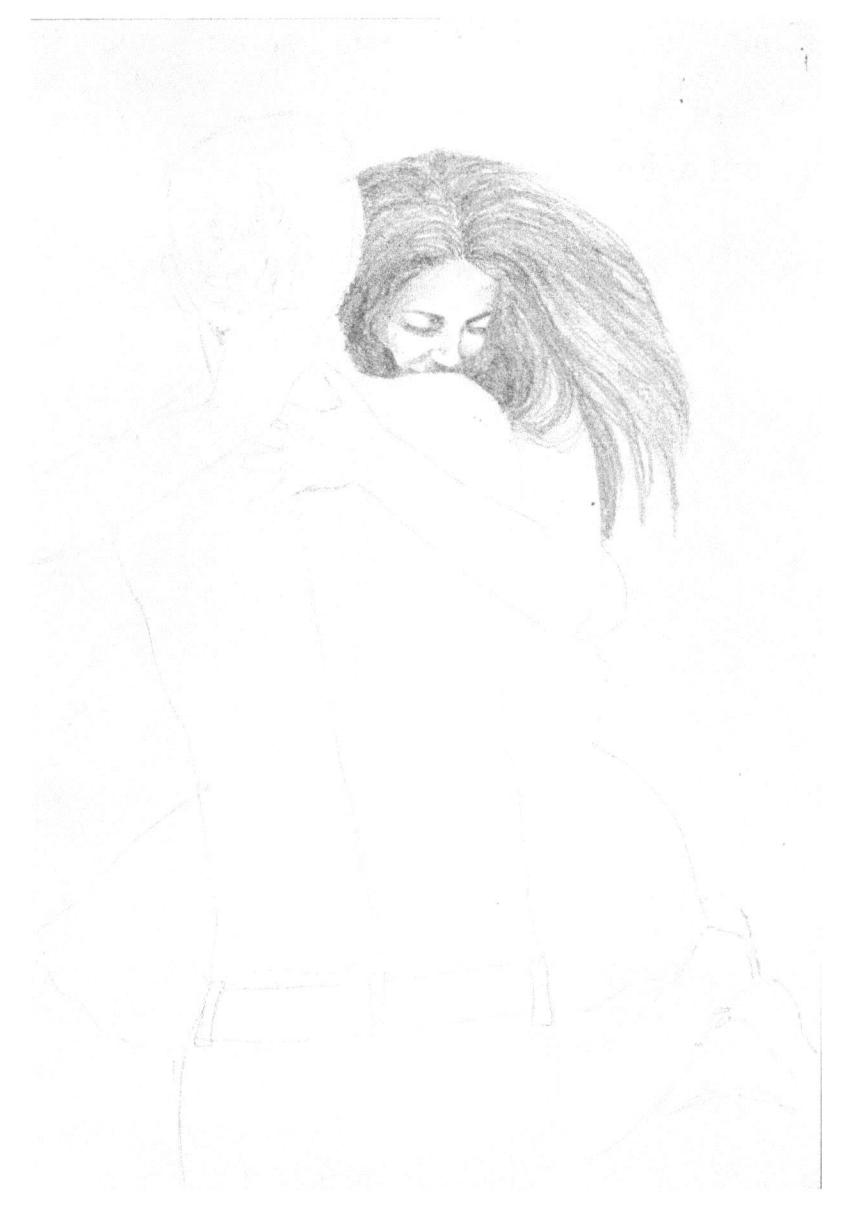

Step 3: Begin with the young lady by sketching out the state of her head. At that point draw in the long

streaming hair. You ought to add some composition to her hair with strand definition. Draw the little ear and point of interest it also.

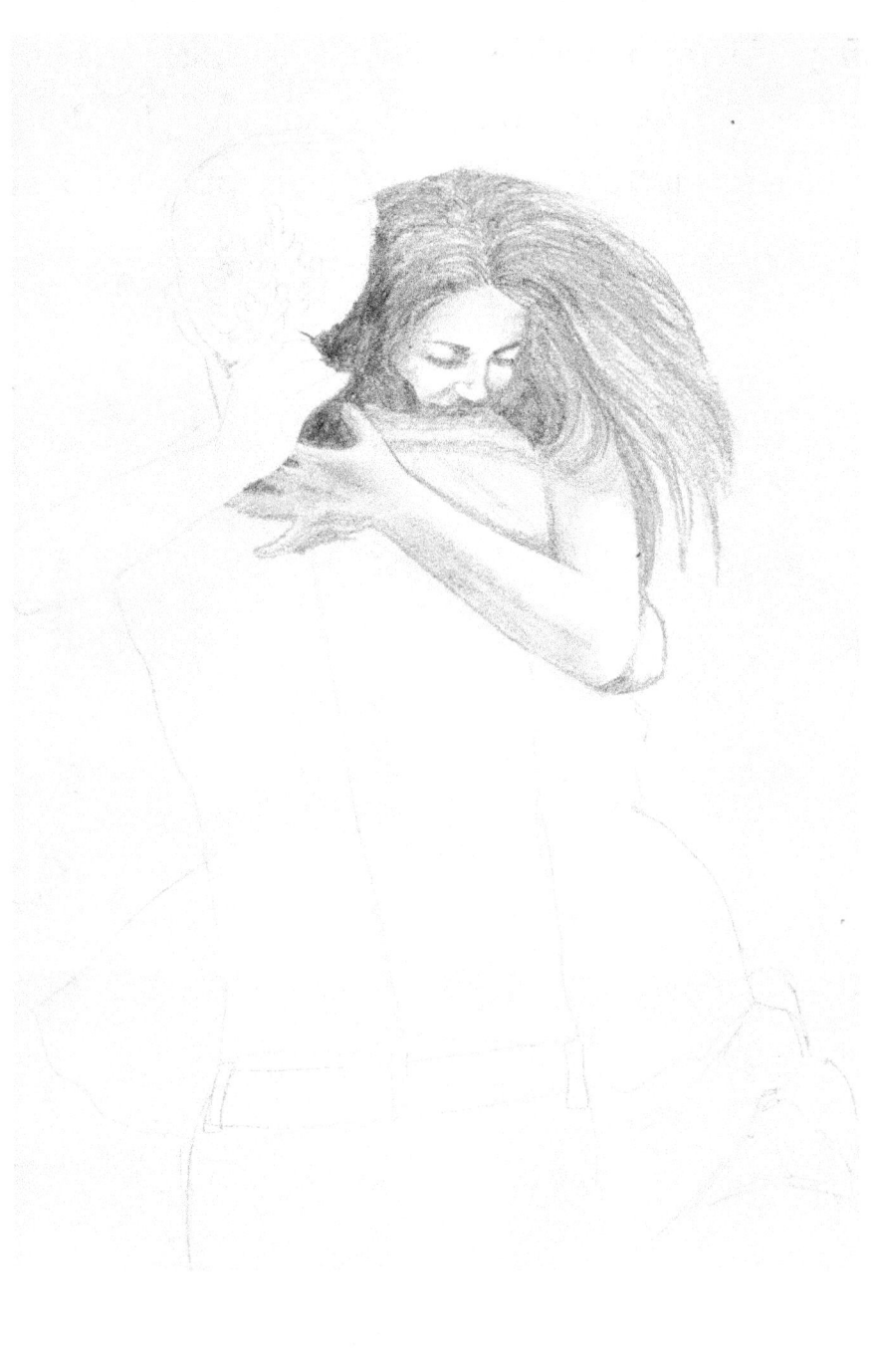

Step 4: In step four we will handle a greater amount of the kid. Start with the jaw line and after that draw the neck, shoulder, arm or sleeve, and after that add specifying to his shirt.

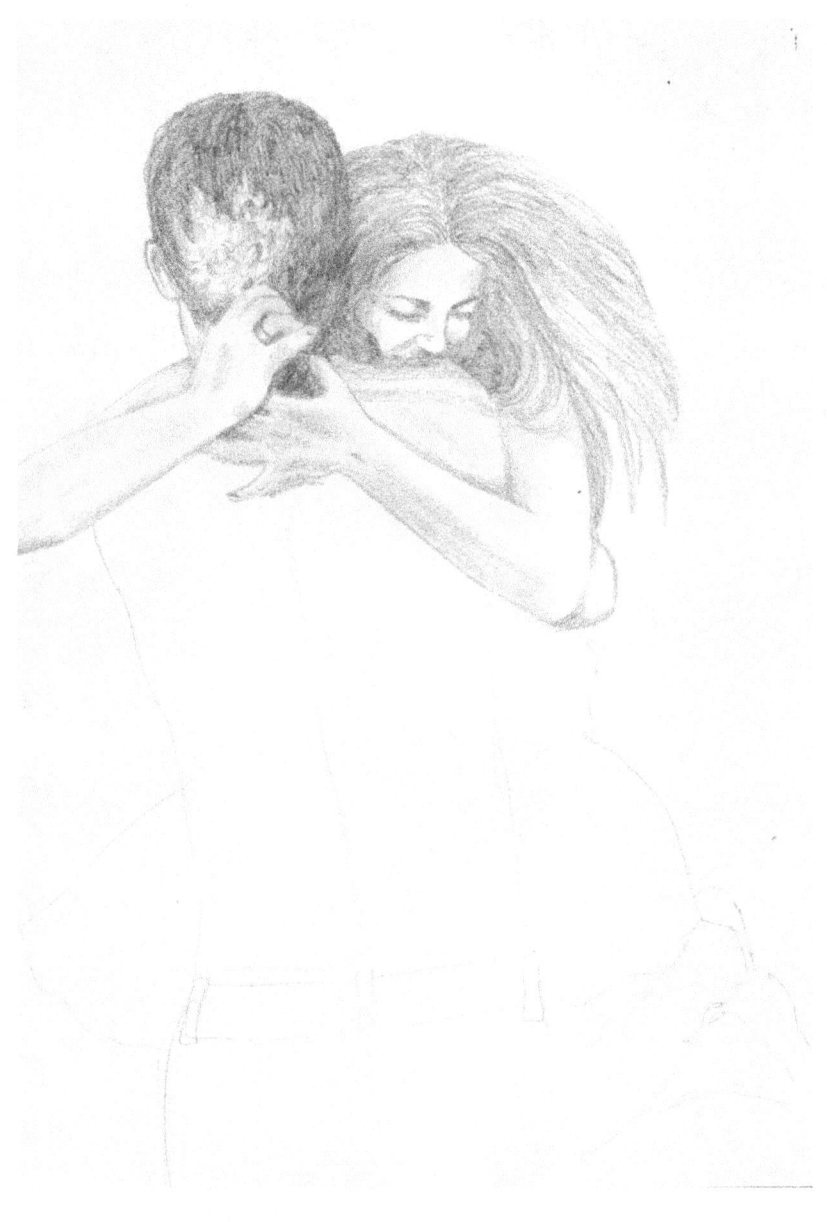

Step 5: Sketch out the state of the young lady's face and after that draw in her eye. Include some become

flushed imprints her cheeks, then include the neck and shoulder.

Step 6: Alright folks, draw the body for your young lady, then draw in her arm which is grasping onto the boy.

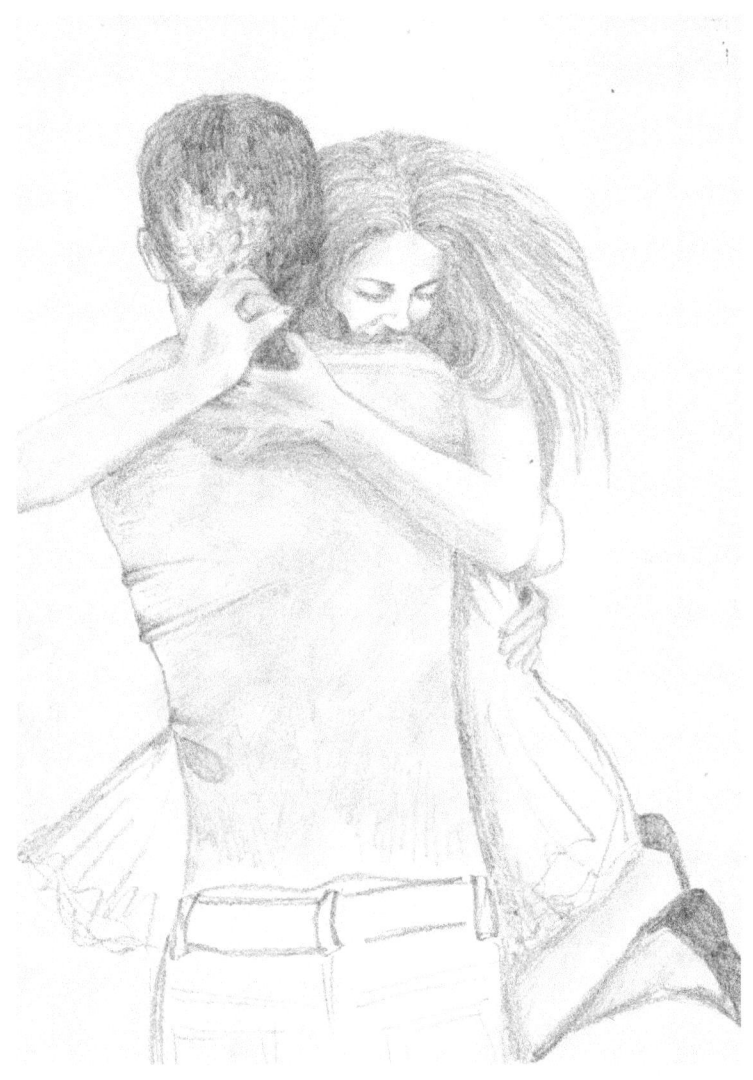

Step 7: For the last drawing step you should simply draw the back of his shirt and include some wrinkle or crinkle. Delete the errors and aides.

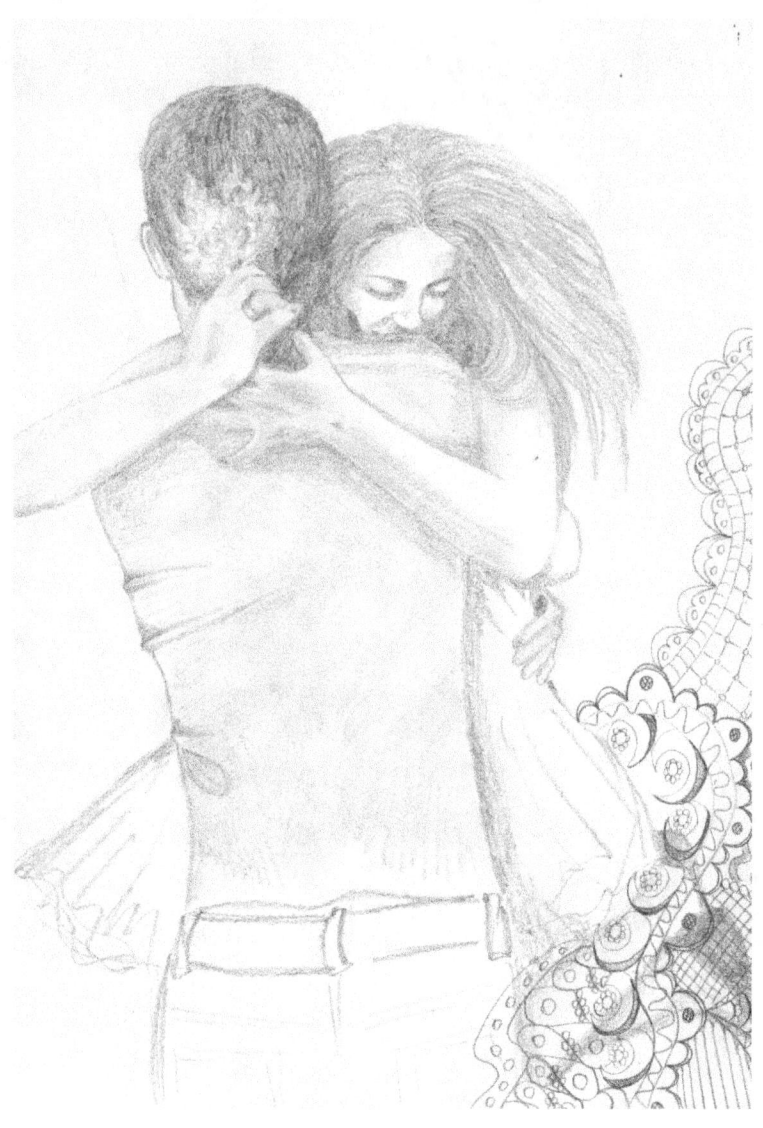

Step 8: That is it, you are all done. Presently you can shading in this couple utilizing your own shades.

Chapter 6 – How to draw a girl kidding a pet

Step 1: This is my tip before you begin on your journey to drawing a girl kissing her pet couple kissing. The most effortless approach to begin these strides is to draw two countenances with one on top of the other and afterward simply delete the lines of the female's nose and top lip.

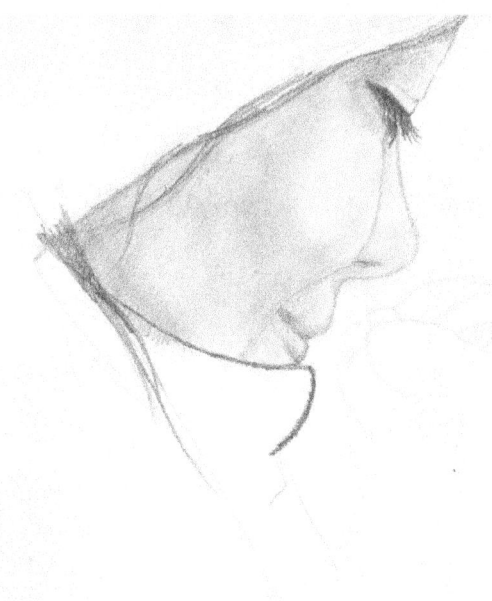

Step 2: Presently in fact this is your initial step and what you will do to begin it off is draw two circles precisely the same for the heads. You will then include the face rules which are two dash like lines and afterward the line of position for their necks.

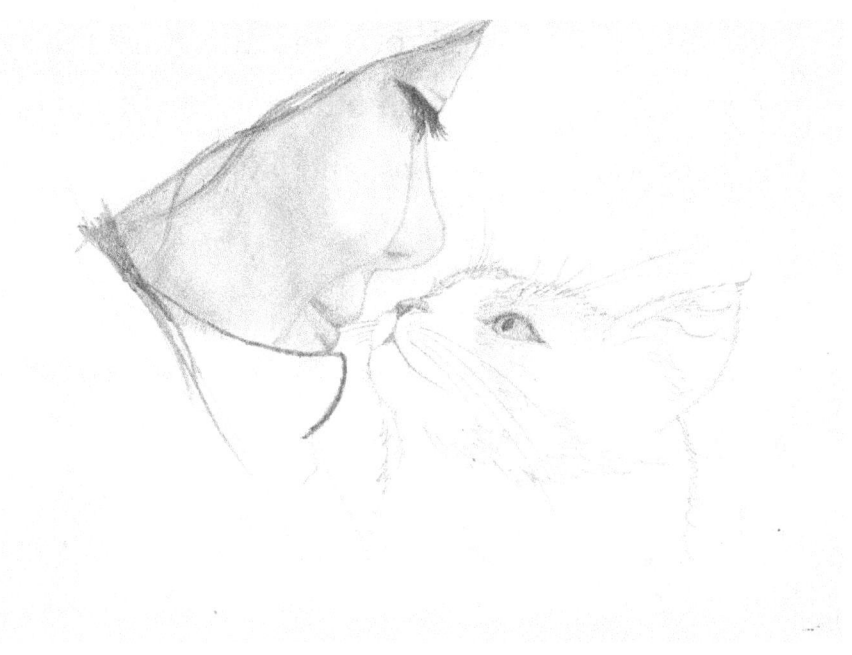

Step 3: In this stride you will begin the sketching procedure of the hairdo in the front and after that the molding of their appearances. When that is done you will draw out and thicken the finished eyes and draw off the front of the necks. Ensure that you curve them fit as a fiddle of a curve.

Step 4: In this fourth step you will begin drawing out whatever remains of the haircut for both the girl kissing her pet female and male. When that is done you will draw out the eyebrows and afterward the eye top shapes. After that sketch out the state of his face which incorporates nose, lips, and jaw.

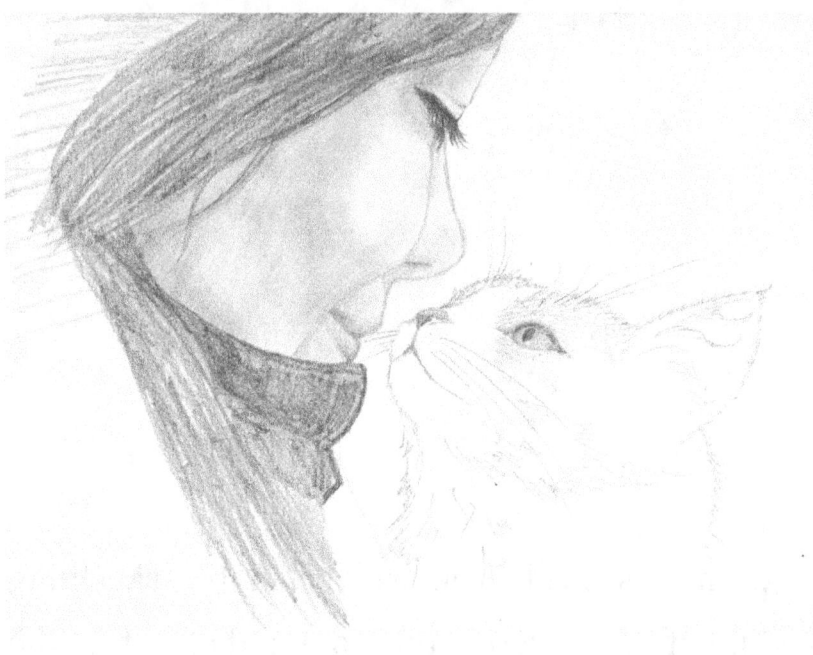

Step 5: Well this is your last drawing step and all you will need to do here is add the hair definition lines to their heads, and after that draw out the state of his ear. When that is done point of interest their cheeks and afterward include a definition line under her button.

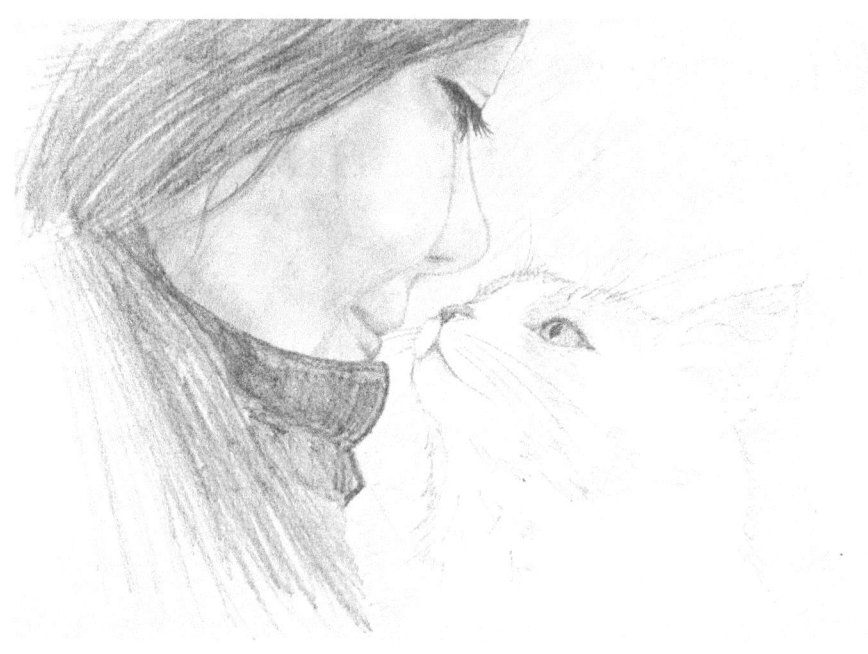

Step 6: When you are done you're drawing ought to turn out resembling the one you see here. All you need to do now is shading them in and give them names.

Chapter 7 – How to draw a girl posing

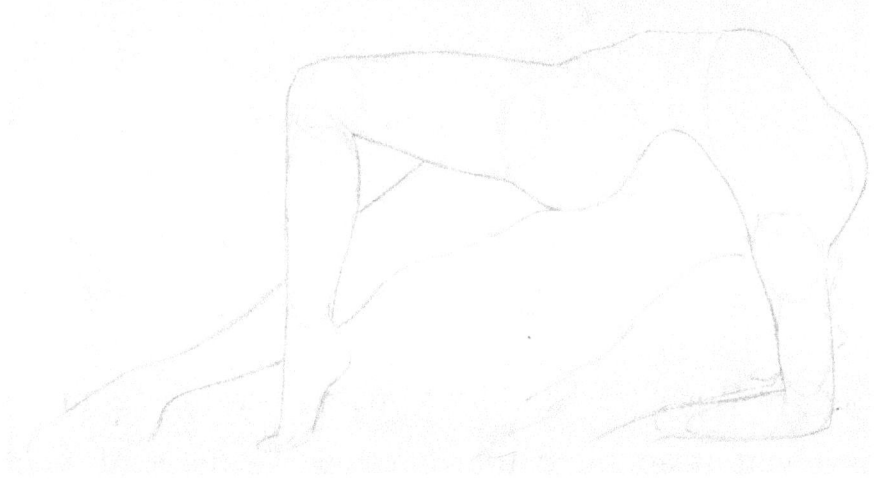

Step 1: Learn how to draw better female figures with the accompanying supportive routines and strategies with the accompanying systems. The accompanying supportive pointers will offer you some assistance with learning how to draw appealing, enthusiastic young ladies and women figures.

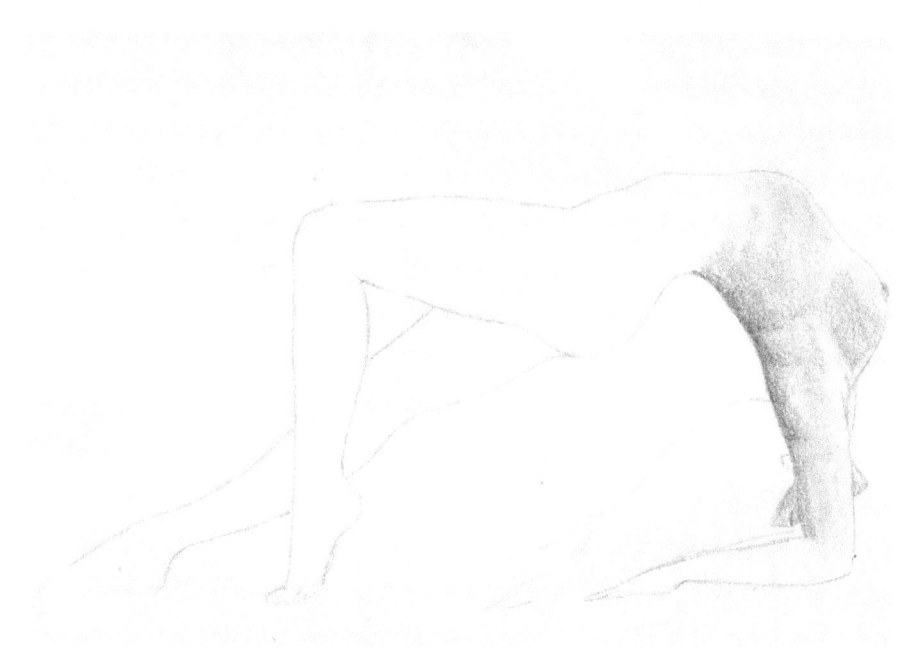

Step 2: On the off chance that we push the jars off of the rack, they turn out to be a great deal all the more fascinating to take a gander at .in light of the fact that they are moving, as well as on the grounds that they now frame a changing, enhanced example.

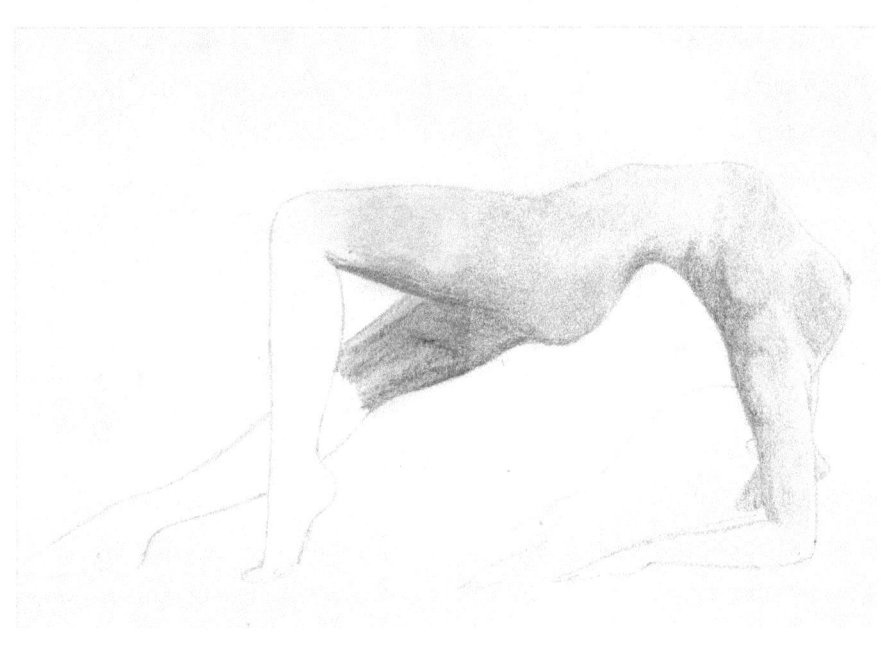

Step 3: The jars that had tumbled off the rack were all the more intriguing to take a gander at. In the same way, the young lady in figure #2 is more satisfying to take a gander at than the young lady that is in figure #1.

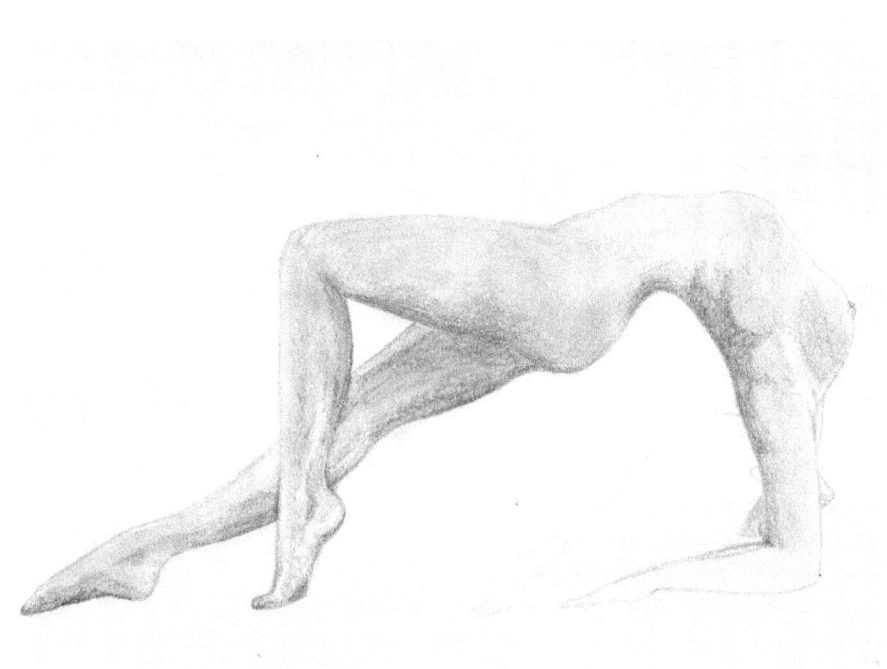

Step 4: The graph above shows how the blueprints of the young lady in figure #2 have been moved marginally to enhance the drawing. Note how the figure #2 young lady's shoulder-line and hip-line are inclined in restricting bearings.

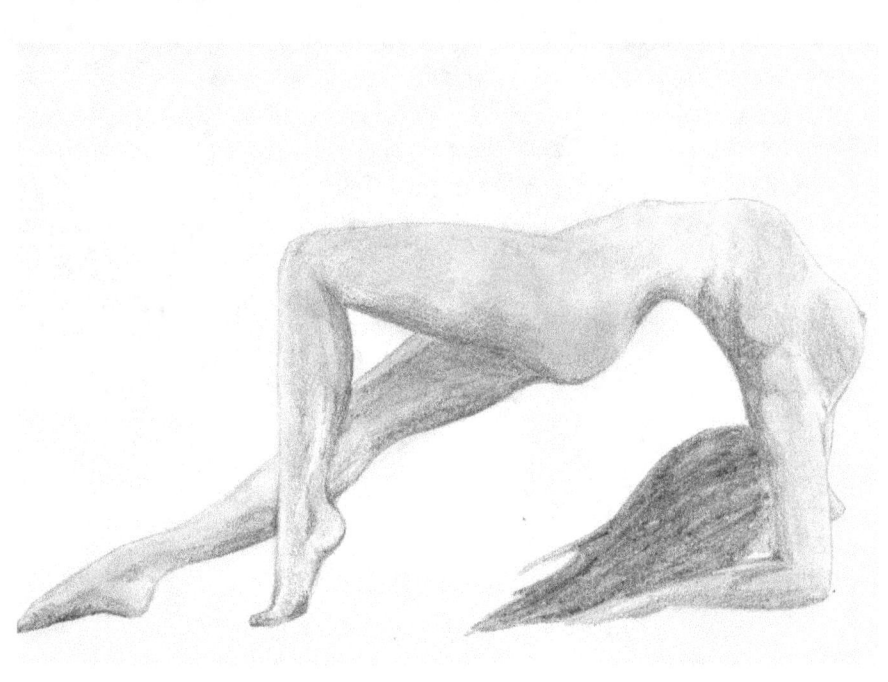

Step 5: Activity in your figure drawings will make them all the more intriguing to take a look at.

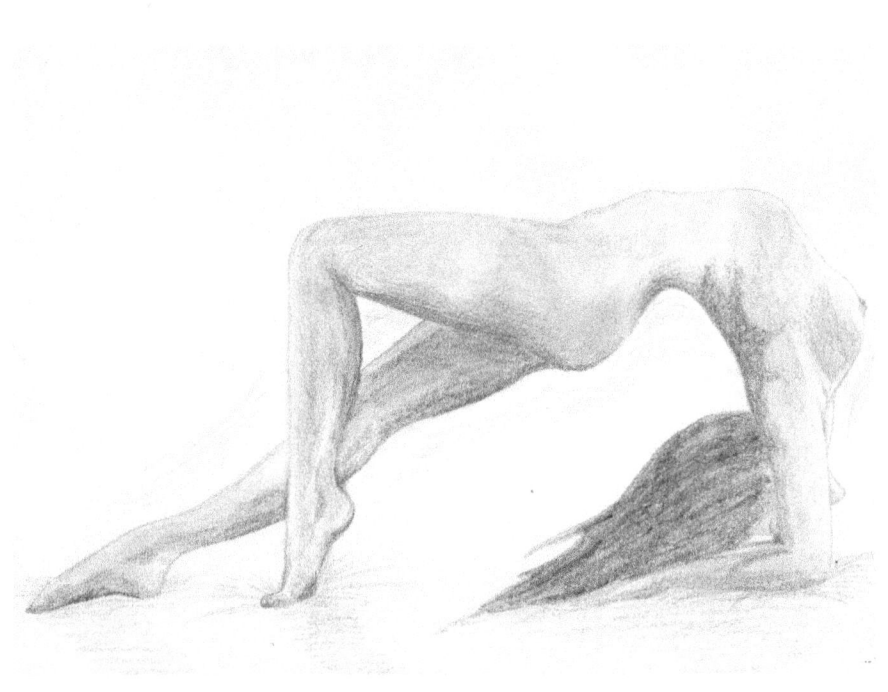

Step 6: This figure is drawn with the goal that it is giving the deception of her being in movement. On the other hand, she is not in movement... she was simply drawn to look as though she was in movement.

Chapter 8 – How to draw a girl kissing

Step 1: Begin with a circle and curves for the heads, and afterward include the rules for both of character's appearances. This will play as the establishment for the characters to fabricate the vital points of interest on. It's likewise the way I began my drawing!

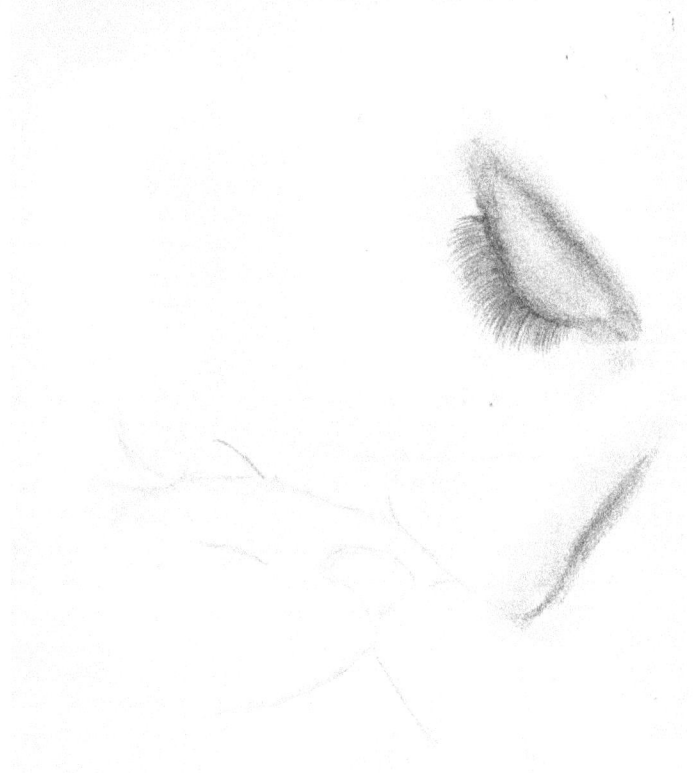

Step 2: Next, work on the aides for the bodies. This may require some an opportunity to chip away at since it's a great deal to draw.

Step 3: Presently characterize the positions of their arms with circles and lines.

Step 4: So now begin to draw the character's arms taking after the lines that you drew on step 3.

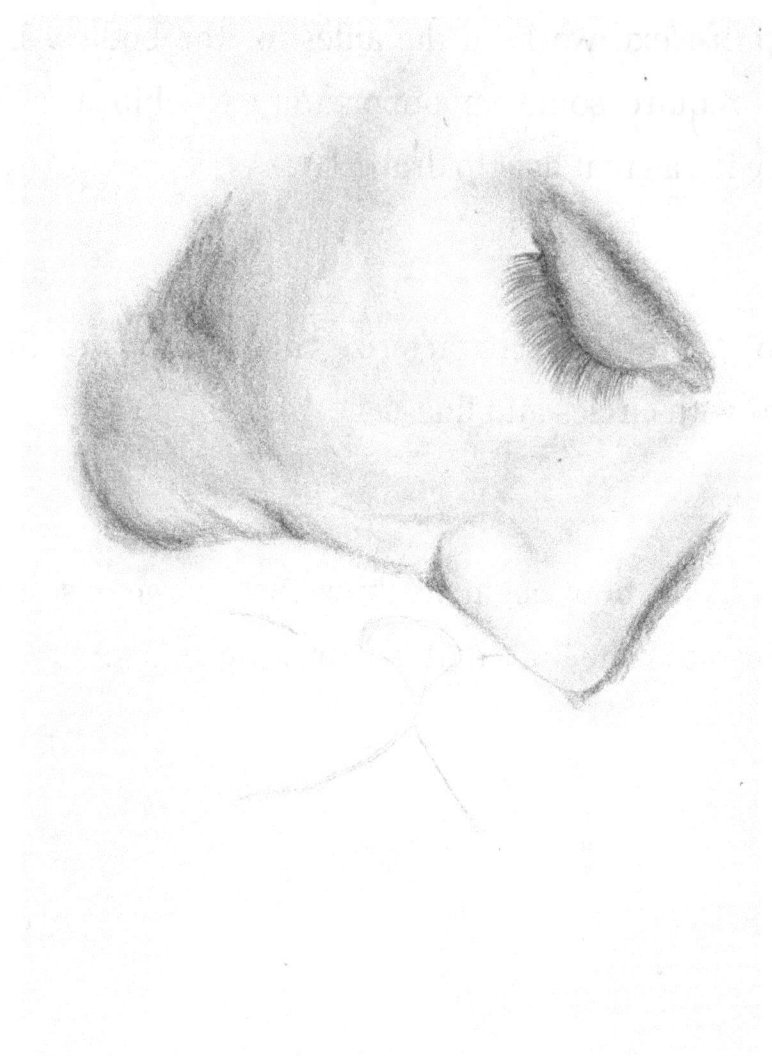

Step 5: This is the thing that your pencil lines ought to look. Before you bounce into cleaning the figures,

eradicate the aides that stray in the middle of the figures.

Step 6: Presently begin to characterize the face's positions, middles and arms, you simply need to line which are obvious parts (blue lines), not every one of the lines that you got from stage 5!

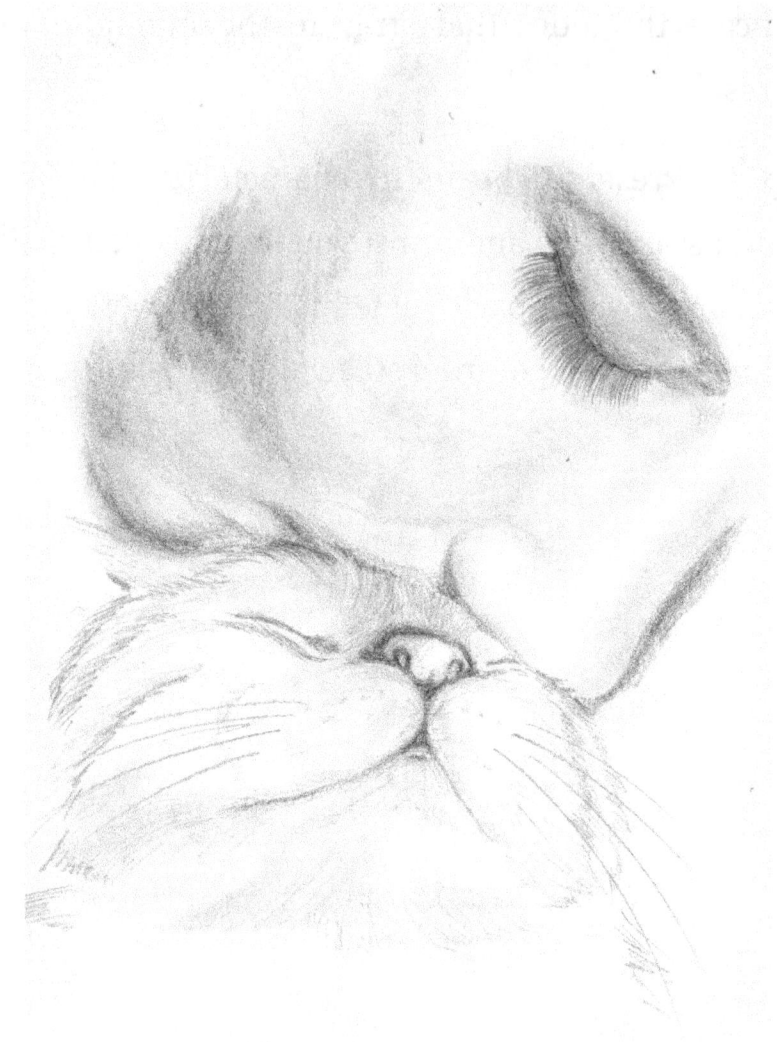

Step 7: Presently, you can begin testing and add facial points of interest and garments to make the characters that are kissing. Perhaps you could include

two young men or possibly two young ladies? Let's turn onto the last step!

Chapter 9 – How to draw a girl kissing 2

Step 1: Here is a little pre-tip before the real drawing steps. The rules won't have the blue profile face and button on the grounds that it discourages the drawing. Just in the event that you require an aide for getting those jaws in. Here it is. The bolts indicate how the jaws are just about on the same curved line.

Step 2: We are taking an alternate route in the rules. Draw the two circles with the long lines for the neck, shoulder and hand. Sketch them with a No. 2 pencil. Keep in mind to do it delicately for simple deletion.

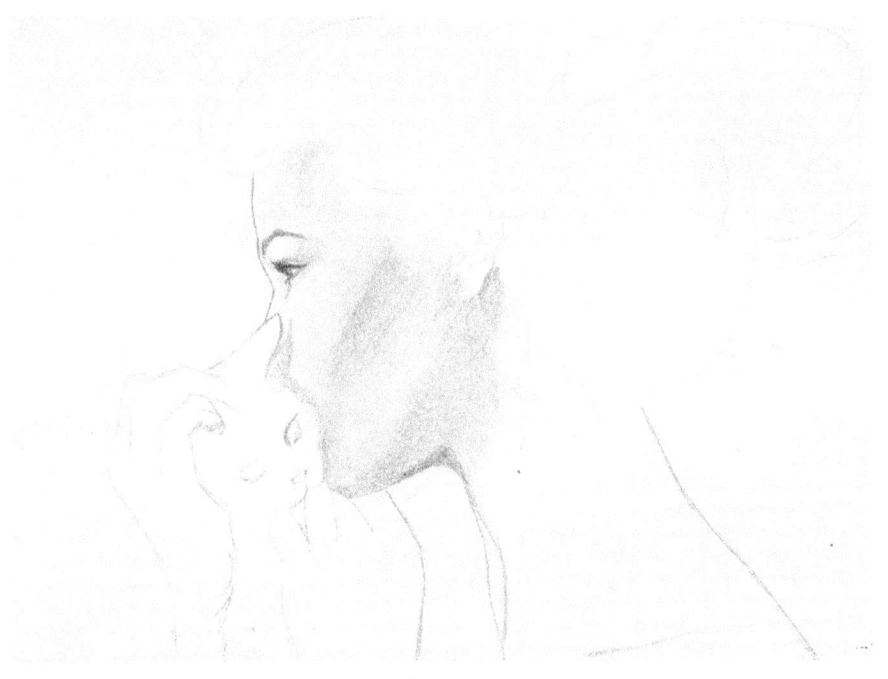

Step 3: You may need to tap on the photo to see where to draw both their eyebrows, eyes and hair. Give a curve to the spiked hair. The circle rules assist you with doing that.

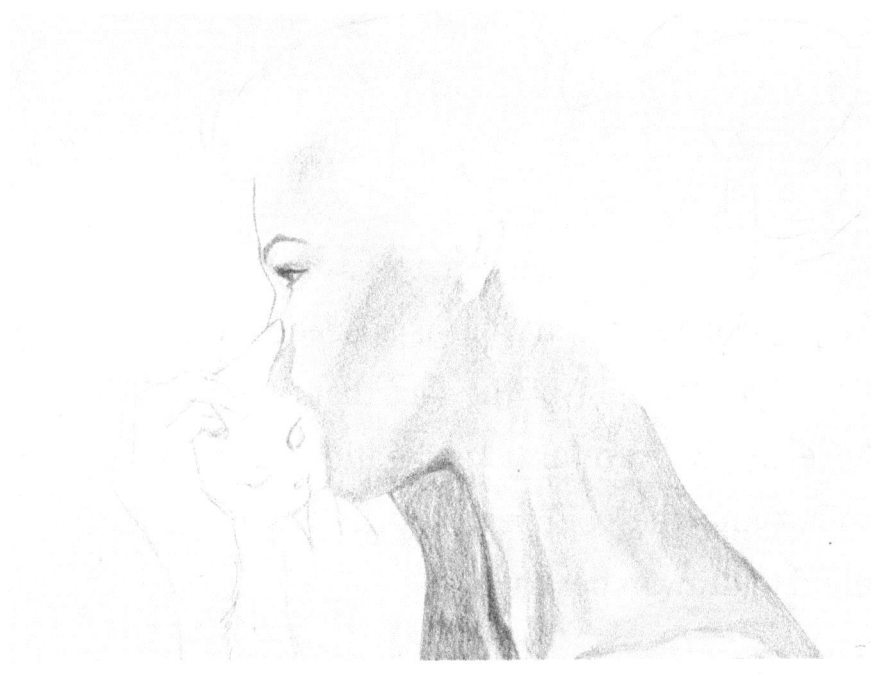

Step 4: Presently draw in their mouths, cheek, jaw line, and necks. Watch nearly where these identify with the rules and draw softly please.

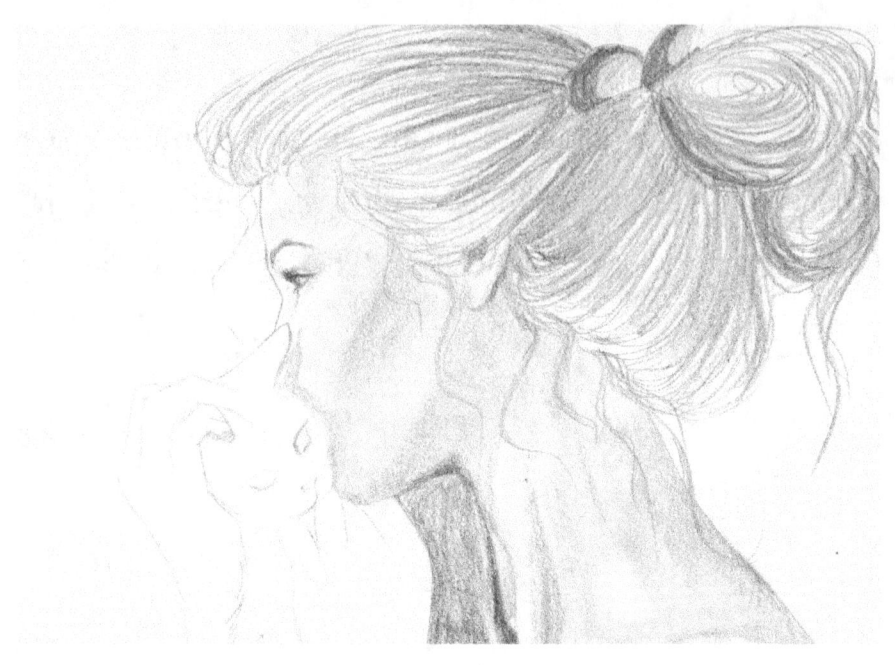

Step 5: Take as much time as is needed while drawing this photo in light of the fact that in this stride you have to give careful consideration to how her hair spikes and the void territory for his hand. Keep in mind to draw in her ear.

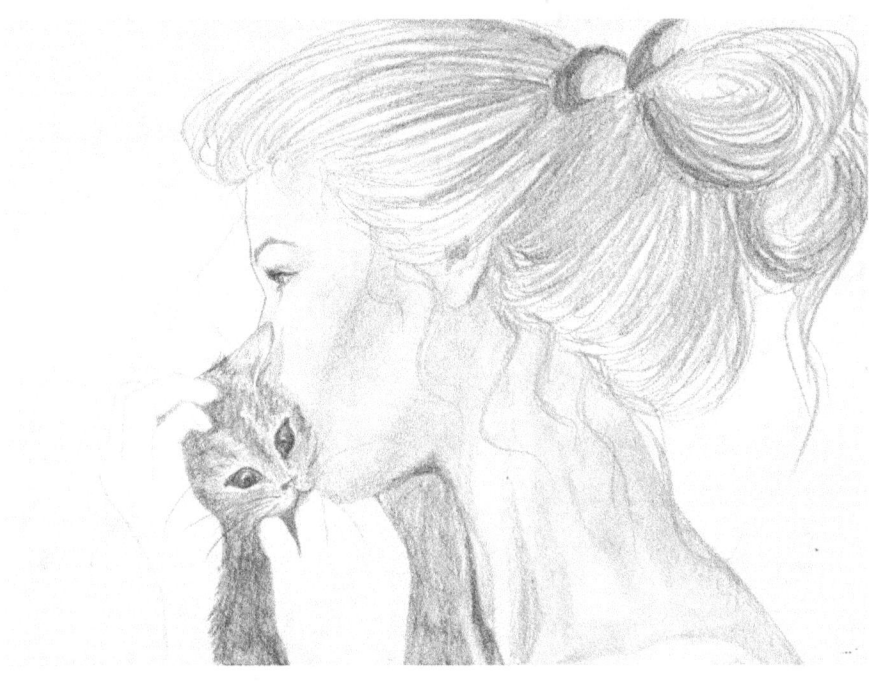

Step 6: Take a stab at looking carefully to where his hair shows up in connection to the rules for more precision. Keep in mind his ear and hair behind it.

Step 7: Presently draw in his grasp holding a lock of her hair and whatever is left of her spiked hair.

Step 8: Draw in whatever is left of his spiked hair, neckline, and shoulder.

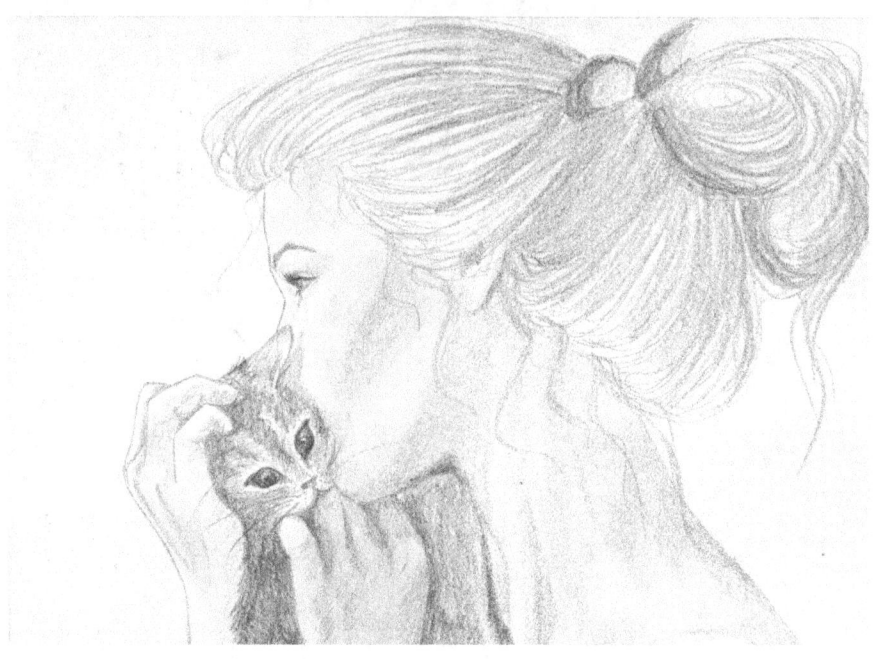

Step 9: You're drawing may resemble this or you may have your own form. As of right now, you can shading in your photo with a medium of your decision.

Conclusion

Drawing eyes can be the hardest part for a craftsman, when attempting to catch the authenticity of the face. Whether it is a pet, a wild creature, a flying creature, or a human, it's all in the eyes.

The eyes are known as the "window to the spirit" by numerous people, and when you have the capacity to catch a feeling on paper, then you have succeeded in breathing life into your piece.

You need to separate the eye into little pieces and after that work on them one by one and develop it in layers, beginning with an unpleasant foundation and afterward building up the layers.

This can be difficult to accomplish from books, or example guidelines, very craftsmen will do definite paint by number units, to get a few thoughts of building and drawing the ideal eye. The same number of paint by number units is done from photos.

Another route is to watch another person draw or paint the ideal eye. You learn from them, and after that practice, and you will then start to shape your own specific manners of drawing and painting, much the same as you have with whatever remains of your piece.

This is an awesome thought, on the off chance that you have room schedule-wise and cash to take lessons, and one on one lessons like that, can cost you a lot of cash, in the event that you go to a gifted craftsman.

On the off chance that like me, you will tend to paint scenes, or inaccessible people or group, to abstain from doing a nearby up of a point by point face, yet once you get it made sense of, and practice you will love drawing eyes.

Never Let Anybody Stifle Your Possible Or Creativity - Regain Your Faith

I used to trust that I am lousy at drawing? I remember getting fear going to Arts courses all through my educating days? The educator is exceptionally furious and at whatever point she talks, it is similar to thunder? When she starts to chide, you can envision the ground underneath her giving way? Land to think about it, I don't remember whenever seeing her grin.

One occurrence left a profound engraving in my psyche? That round, we were? Expected to draw and paint anything related to the ocean? We were educated to locate a suitable picture and repeat it.? I had a troublesome time? I remember I was in any case chipping away at the drawing at around 2am to 3am in the early morning of the due date? I felt baffled and as I battled back again my tears, I sprinkled dark paint everywhere throughout the drawing? There was a little sampan in the ocean? The sky was dull? The ocean was significantly darker and stormier? The waves were undermining? It was raining extraordinarily with electrical discharges? The winds were wailing? It was an unnerving sight.

In spite of the fact that I didn't admission too seriously for that bit of fine art, I began to hate Arts? It was a torment going to Arts classes? My drawings were solid and dead? I continued letting myself know that I was really poor at drawing? That I was not by any means ready to draw straightforward questions acceptably.

By the by, I created a lovely disclosure as of late? I have more often than not been captivated with kid's shows? The adorable Disney characters? The toon bear? The toon man? The toon animals? The toon creatures? A wide range of kid's shows? 1 day, out of the blue, a little voice whispered to me, "Why not see how to draw kid's shows?"? Without a great deal thought, I responded,"I am lousy at drawing? I can in no way, shape or form draw."

Abnormally, a few days after the fact, I surfed the web on toon drawing and discovered an intriguing site that shows toon drawing on-line.? I received the headings and was charmingly amazed that I could draw stick fellow, wood gentleman and frankfurter fellow? In spite of the fact that these are fundamental degree drawings and don't call for much drawing ability, I truly feel greatly pleased with my expert things.

Can you think it?? Some person who has, for quite a long time, lost confidence in drawing can at last draw something tolerable?? Presently I am sure that with practice, I will be in a position to draw vastly improved? How credulous of me to have conveyed the accepted for quite a long time that I can't draw and deny myself of this sort of colossal joy and profound satisfaction.

Have you whenever been informed that you are miserable at something?? Have you ever been informed that you are not diminishing out for an assignment?? Have you by a few means lost confidence subsequent to having experienced some awful experiences?? On the off chance that your answer is useful, do have second accepted? Re-take a gander at the circumstance? Be open to probability as the truth may end up being or disaster will be imminent.